spent

s p e n t

MEMOIRS *of a* SHOPPING ADDICT

AVIS CARDELLA

Little, Brown and Company

New York   Boston   London

Little, Brown and Company
Hachette Book Group
237 Park Avenue, New York, NY 10017
www.hachettebookgroup.com

First Edition: May 2010

Little, Brown and Company is a division of Hachette Book Group, Inc.
The Little, Brown name and logo are trademarks of Hachette Book Group, Inc.

The author is grateful for permission to reprint material from
The Soul of the New Consumer by David Lewis and Darren Bridger,
Nicholas Brealey Publishing © 2000, 2001.

Library of Congress Cataloging-in-Publication Data
Cardella, Avis.
  Spent : memoirs of a shopping addict / by Avis Cardella. — 1st ed.
    p. cm.
  Includes bibliographical references.
  ISBN 978-0-316-03560-6
  1. Cardella, Avis. 2. Compulsive shopping — United States —
Case studies. 3. Addicts — United States — Biography. 4. Shopping —
United States — Psychological aspects — Case studies. 5. Consumption
(Economics) — United States — Psychological aspects — Case studies.
6. Shopping — Social aspects — United States — Case studies. 7. Consumption
(Economics) — Social aspects — United States — Case studies. I. Title.
  RC569.5.S56C37 2010
  362.196'85840092 — dc22   2009038527
  [B]

658.834 (Cardella)
NOB

10 9 8 7 6 5 4 3 2 1

RRD-IN

Printed in the United States of America

For my mother and father

CONTENTS

AUTHOR'S NOTE

Spent is a work of nonfiction. Certain names and identifying details have been changed.

spent

One

BARNEYS, BERGDORF'S, BLOOMINGDALE'S

❧❦

I used shopping to avoid myself. I used shopping to define myself. And at some point, I realized that I was no longer consuming; I was just being consumed. When I stood in the lingerie department of Barneys, flanked by rows of candy-colored Cosabella thongs and Ripcosa tank tops, and couldn't remember how I got there, I knew I was in trouble.

That was back at the turn of the millennium, when life couldn't have been better, but when I knew that something was going terribly wrong. Why was I standing in Barneys in a stupor? Why was I buying twenty pairs of underwear?

"Can I help you?" said the salesperson.

"Yes, I want one in every color."

And then the walk home, the strange feeling of not wanting what I now had: twenty Cosabella thongs wrapped in whisper-thin tissue paper at the bottom of a black Barneys shopping bag.

I returned to my apartment and threw the bag in the back of the closet, where other discarded purchases were already marooned.

But, by all appearances, life was good. I was living in Manhattan and had a career as a freelance writer. I was engaged to a wealthy European businessman, and we had two homes, two cars, and an abundance of friends. My closet was full of beautiful things to wear, and there were all kinds of places to wear them.

It was the late 1990s—the age of "irrational exuberance"—and everyone was irrational; everyone was exuberant; everyone was shopping. Why not me? What could be wrong with that? Shopping almost felt mandatory in Manhattan. Just outside my front door was a veritable candy land: Tiffany's, Chanel, Louis Vuitton, Manolo Blahnik, Bulgari, Takashimaya, Bonwit Teller, Prada, Linda Dresner, Emporio Armani, Tod's, Nike, Burberry's—and my three favorite department stores: Barneys, Bergdorf's, and Bloomingdale's.

Let me give the geography because junkies are always concerned with logistics: Bergdorf's was the closest of my beloved retail fixes, about a six-minute walk from the luxury high-rise tower in which I lived. Barneys was next, about a ten-minute walk depending on the route I'd take. Bloomingdale's could be reached in fifteen minutes at a good clip.

Of the three, Barneys on Madison Avenue was the one I liked best. Barneys was modern, fresh, and white walled. Stepping into Barneys always felt a bit like boarding a spaceship. Sometimes I felt there was a distinct atmospheric change, a subtle barometric shift that seemed to occur in the small vestibule that led from the street to the store. Consequently, everything for sale at Barneys carried an aura of specialness, even otherworldliness. When I was strolling alone around Barneys, the world outside ceased to exist.

I could spend hours anchored in the shoe department. The salesman knew me by name. I knew his too. John had been selling me shoes for years. We first met when he was working at the downtown Barneys on 17th Street. It goes back that far, perhaps to the late eighties. He was always friendly and seemed to enjoy his job, but what he really wanted to do was bake cookies. I confided that I wanted to become a writer.

This is what happens when you spend a lot of time shopping: You get to know sales associates, and they get to know you. Sometimes you end up receiving handwritten notes in the mail, informing you of the arrival of a new collection or inviting you to a private sale. You get Christmas cards too.

At Bergdorf's I never knew anybody on the selling floor by name. I liked to float through the store and not speak. I felt intimidated there and slightly out of my league. Pretending to be born and bred Bergdorf's was something of a private fantasy for me. It must have been a New York thing. I didn't enjoy shopping at Bergdorf's as much as at Barneys, but Bergdorf's had an air of superiority. Even pushing my way through the heavy, gilded revolving door felt like an initiation rite. Getting my hair cut and colored on the light-filled top floor at the John Barrett Salon was the closest I ever came to feeling like the "real deal": a Bergdorf blonde.

At Bloomingdale's I could indulge my most secret self. I had a history at Bloomingdale's because that is where I had shopped with my mother and where I could always return to dive into the folds of my past. As I came to realize, my shopping habit had deep roots. The memory of shopping with my mother is a touchstone.

I used shopping to avoid myself.

At the end of the twentieth century, as the Y2K bug was threatening to sour the big party, as New York's dot-com bubble was growing and Wall Street mavericks were riding roughshod through town, guns blazing, I was waking up from my big sleep, my stupor, my sidestepping grief.

Who was I?

I was a woman living in Manhattan. I was a creature with a cultivated appearance. Everything about me was carefully calibrated. Tips and cues were dictated by the pages of fashion magazines; I tried to follow them meticulously. My regimen included Pilates classes, yoga, and core fusion. The resulting body was taut and toned, rope muscled and fine. My skin also was polished and buffed like a brand-new automobile; it caught the light and glowed. This was the expensive appearance, the shopper's appearance, because shopping was an essential part of the lifestyle. If you didn't look the part, the sales associates wouldn't take you seriously. It was the acceptable appearance, because on any given day, as the sun came slanting down New York's grid of corridors, hundreds of women who looked just like me could be seen scampering to and fro clutching shopping bags.

Looking back, I realize that I must have joined that team as a sleepwalker. At the time, I had no recollection of how I got there. I only know that I awoke one day to find my closet filled with the right kinds of suits—Prada, Armani, Calvin Klein, Jil Sander—and the right kinds of shoes with heart-stabbing heels, the type that made my legs look just right, like magic. (It's all about illusion.) And in my bathroom cabinet, there were the right kinds of creams: the Laszlo Night Serum, the Crème de la Mer, the regenerating fluid, the Clinique soap, the vitamin C rejuvenating gel, the whitening toothpaste, and the amino acids with strange-sounding names.

I awoke one day with the realization that the only way I could have acquired all these accoutrements of the cultivated appearance was by having shopped for them. Therefore, I must have been shopping for a *very* long time.

So that is how, one glorious, sunny Tuesday afternoon, I found myself in Barneys and couldn't remember how I got there. Where I should have been was home finishing a story about the fashion photographer Michael Thompson. I had interviewed Thompson at a downtown studio where he was photographing Halle Berry for Revlon. It was my prize interview, hard-won from the clutches of another writer. But now the story was overdue, and I...well, I was standing awe-struck in the lingerie department.

I was staring at the Cosabella panties.

There must have been twenty colors or even more. There

were so many delectable colors: Tang orange, bubble gum pink, grape, lemon, Astroturf green, lipstick red, fuchsia, lavender, blush, and café au lait. Some Ripcosa tank tops in white and black were dangling from a railing just above the panties, and I asked for three of those. "Two in black and one in white, please."

Thongs and tanks—an army of undies surrounded me. There were also brassieres and bustiers, camisoles and cotton pajama tops, satin lounging robes and silk tap pants. And it was all there to be bought. I was there to buy. That's where I was when I should have been at home working.

I watched as the salesperson carefully checked the label of each pair of panties, and I felt as if a helium balloon was being inflated inside my head. It took up the space where my brain was supposed to be. I could have floated to the ceiling and stayed there for an eternity, hovering above the lingerie department, because I felt a kind of high at the thought of purchasing all those panties.

But as I walked home that day, I wasn't sure what I wanted anymore. I only knew that I was slipping. It was impossible to imagine how far the slide would be or how hard the landing. I definitely didn't know where it would end. I only knew that I had started to experience something troubling and inexplicable.

What was this shopping itch that had begun to appear with regularity? It was like an alien being that tapped into my psyche and told me to stop everything I was doing in order to shop. Even though shopping was a routine part of my life, this itch felt different. It demanded to be scratched.

When the itch would return, the only thing to relieve it was a purchase. I had begun to shop like someone on autopilot, purchasing impulsively, mindlessly. These shopping episodes were followed by regret and sadness—sometimes so profound that I couldn't breathe, as if something heavy had settled on my chest and couldn't be moved.

I had loved shopping since I was a young girl. What could be wrong with shopping? When I was in my teens, it hardly seemed possible that something as pleasurable, as innocuous—one of the most ordinary of pastimes—could wreak havoc with my life.

When I got home that day, I opened my closet door and was confronted with the contents. There were my beautiful suits, my columns of cashmere sweaters, stacks of T-shirts and summer dresses. Everything was in its place. But at the back of the closet, there was a growing pile of unopened shopping bags. One bag contained a $500 denim jacket; another had three pairs of yoga pants. I threw in the glossy black bag from Barneys and shut the door.

Shopping was my escape, my friend, my balm, my release, my pacifier, my pleasure, my secret, my pastime, my kill time, my fantasy, my reality, my recreation, my therapy, my drug, my stimulant, my lover, my memory, my link with the past, my trip to the future.

Was it also my addiction?

Two

ONIOMANIA AND ME

O niomania is the clinical name for the compulsive desire to shop. While it may seem like a recent phenomenon, the term was coined by German psychiatrist Emil Kraepelin in 1915. The word *shopaholic* dates back to 1984, having first appeared in an article in the *Washington Post,* defending Diana, Princess of Wales, who was rumored to have had an excessive shopping habit. The article vehemently dismissed such speculation as "absolute rubbish." It wasn't until 1991 that the term *compulsive shopper* came into use. And in 1995 *extreme shopper* showed up in print.

When I first started reading about compulsive shopping in various books and magazines, I was surprised to learn that Mary Todd Lincoln was a shopping addict. It has been said that she purchased eighty-four pairs of gloves in less than a month.

History, it turns out, is sprinkled with famous shopping personalities from Marie Antoinette to Imelda Marcos and William Randolph Hearst. Another first lady, Jacqueline

Kennedy, was also known for such indulgences, particularly in French fashion. In a letter to French couturier Oleg Cassini, she expresses a wish for the designer to dress her but explains that she doesn't want to become a modern Marie Antoinette or be "plagued by fashion stories of a sensational nature" or be seen to be "buying too much." Kennedy may have had good reason to be coy. She was committed to wearing American-made fashion, but her love of French couture could have been perceived as a betrayal.

Today, celebrities routinely discuss their excessive purchases with little concern about being judged. Victoria Beckham is said to be a self-confessed shopaholic who flaunts her collection of more than one hundred Hermès handbags. Actresses such as Sarah Jessica Parker, Kate Hudson, and Lindsay Lohan are noted for owning hundreds of pairs of jeans and shoes. And Serena Williams sounds distinctly modern when she recounts her battle with compulsive online shopping in a 2001 interview with CBC Sports. Williams admits to having shopped online for up to six hours a day. "Every day I was in my room, and I was online," she told CBC. "I wasn't able to stop, and I bought, bought, bought, bought, bought."

Still, the most intriguing compulsive shopper may have been Andy Warhol. "Buying is much more American than thinking," he wrote. He embodied this philosophy, regularly enlisting friends to accompany him to sales, auctions, flea markets, and department stores. He even enjoyed hearing about other people's shopping trips, often requesting details: where, what, when, and why.

When he died in 1987, hundreds of shopping bags

containing things that had never been used or worn were found in his apartment. And in 1989 Simon Doonan, creative director of Barneys, paid homage to Warhol the compulsive shopper by re-creating a portion of his posthumously discovered stash for the windows of the trendy department store. Doonan's display featured, among other things, Barbie dolls, vintage pornographic magazines, cookie jars, and an avalanche of shopping bags. In 1997, almost a full decade later, Doonan was asked to reproduce the window display for The Warhol Look / Glamour, Style, Fashion exhibition at New York's Whitney Museum of American Art.

What could be so compelling about the detritus of Warhol's shopaholic habits?

To my mind, Warhol seemed to instinctively understand the importance of "stuff" in American culture. He had described department stores as museums and expressed his belief that the people who had the biggest fame were those who had their names on stores. "The people with very big stores named after them are the ones I'm really jealous of," he wrote.

Warhol's art and shopping revolved around the fluid nature of identity and a desire for transcendence. My own relationship to shopping, with all its implications of going beyond one's ordinary boundaries, may have represented a tangible link to that desire.

◆ ◆ ◆

My first memorable shopping trip was to downtown Brooklyn's Abraham & Straus department store to purchase bell-bottom trousers. I was seven years old. My grandmother, a consummate gift giver, was taking me on this shopping adventure along with my best friend Christine. The trip culminated in the purchase of two identical pairs of plaid wool bell-bottoms: one for me, one for Christine. On the bus ride home I remember clutching the bag in my tiny fist.

If it's true that all addicts store up their firsts—first sip, first snort, first bet—then maybe this shopping trip registers as a first for me. It was a moment so rich with meaning that decades later, at age thirty-eight, I would find myself standing in a downtown Manhattan clothing boutique, transfixed by a pair of bell-bottom trousers, in a plaid of autumnal shades, in wool, just like my first memorable pair. I would have to buy them.

Our family of five lived in a small apartment in Fort Greene, Brooklyn. Space always seemed to be tight, and so was money. I wasn't aware of being either rich or poor, but I knew that I had to share a bedroom with my brothers Francis and Stephan, and that this had something to do with the fact that we couldn't afford a larger apartment. I would have preferred to have a bedroom of my own.

My brothers were typical boys, and I, being the youngest, often ended up taking the brunt of their rambunctious behavior. They tried to suffocate me with pillows and make me their slave. Stephan, the eldest, forced me to feed him grapes and massage his feet. Francis, who was only a year older than me, was less demanding and more of an accomplice for me. Together we enjoyed some mischievous moments, but most of the time I was quiet and tried to keep to myself.

My withdrawal wasn't only to seek refuge from my brothers.

In addition to getting my first memorable trousers at the age of seven, I was diagnosed with a condition known as amblyopia, or "lazy eye," and given a prescription for glasses—and a black eye patch, like a pirate's. From that point on, I became isolated and sought refuge in books and in my clothes.

I cannot think back to that time without remembering the force with which the ocular accessories changed my feelings about myself. To my seven-year-old mind, they instantly rendered me homely, like a reverse fairy tale: the swan that turns into the ugly duckling. One day I was a pretty little girl, the next I was a freak, teased mercilessly at school and even at home. "Men never make passes at girls who wear glasses," my father taunted, oblivious to the trauma those words stirred in me. Would no man want to marry me? What would I do? If I could not be a wife, what would I become?

The person I wanted to become was my mother. My mother entranced me. She was tall, elegant, and always seemed to be dressed for a costume party. Her clothes were exquisite and sometimes exotic. There is a photograph of me—around age eight—gazing with admiration at my mother, who was dressed like a Russian princess. In the photo, she is wearing a white satin blouse with a Cossack neck, and her hands are clasped inside a fur muff. In another photo, she is dressed like a barmaid in a saloon, her long black hair piled high on her head, and her petticoat hiked to reveal a satin garter. I also remember her wearing an orange Betsey Johnson blouse with a moon-and-stars print. She wore that blouse with black satin palazzo pants. She would prance around the apartment in those pants, which seemed wide enough to sweep the floors. But the apartment was small and the pants were large, and they made her seem too big to fit in the confines of the space.

In a spool of memories I keep of my mother, I see her warmth and love and patience. She was kind and sensitive to my needs but not always with me. She was physically present, but there was something about her that remained remote, impossible to reach. I felt I was forever bumping against this impossibility, as if it were an actual barrier, a wall of glass.

Today, when I read accounts from therapists who explain that compulsive disorders (one of which is shopping addiction) may be linked to some lack in the earliest stages of development, perhaps even infancy, I wonder if this doesn't concern my own history. Did my mother's remoteness represent such a lack? The kind of lack that those same therapists say can lead to an emotional emptiness that can only be assuaged by shopping?

I remember my mother constantly buying me clothing, but this can't be entirely true. My father was a blue-collar worker, an installer for AT&T, and his paycheck didn't allow for such extravagances. My mother was a homemaker.

Yet, even in photographs, I see myself as a well-dressed child. But perhaps I have infused my wardrobe with extra meaning, thinking of it as an important link between my mother and me.

Her taste in clothing was sophisticated and refined, and this didn't always sit well with me. For my First Holy Communion, I wanted a frothy concoction, a dress with petticoats, ribbons, and lace. My mother insisted on a simple column dress in white crystal-pleated chiffon. Years later, I would look at that dress and appreciate its elegance, but at the time I felt like a loser. There I was, wearing a dress that fell to my knees in a tragic straight line, while all the other girls wore elaborate confections.

For Easter, she bought me beautiful spring coats; one in champagne-colored silk faille with a paisley-print lining is etched in my mind.

My mother had always picked out clothing for me, but when we finally moved from the apartment in Brooklyn to a house on Staten Island, I wanted to choose my own things. My tastes weren't as refined as my mother's. I insisted on a bright kelly green wrap coat that I wore with an equally garish green beret. For my friend Diane's birthday party, I picked out a white angel-sleeved blouse, ruched at the bodice, and paired it with grape-colored crushed-velvet hot pants. At the party, I felt sassy enough to take off my glasses, gossip about boys, and sing aloud to Tony Orlando and Dawn's "Knock Three Times." And then, there were the

Pocahontas-style knee-high suede boots that I spotted in the window of Thom McAn. I begged my mother to buy them for my birthday. She did. They were presented in a large, unwieldy box. I was ecstatic.

Among this clutch of memorable shopping trips and their bounty, there was only one bad moment. The day our family was due to embark on a summer vacation, my mother realized that I needed a new swimsuit. She asked my father to take me to a children's clothing store, a mom-and-pop place that I felt I'd definitely outgrown. I was eleven and starting to develop. I did not want to buy a bathing suit at the kiddie shop, nor did I want my father to oversee the purchase.

As a child, I found my father aloof, authoritative, and inscrutable. As far back as I can remember, he wore tinted eyeglasses that seemed to exaggerate his air of mystery. I was always trying to look into my father's eyes, to gauge what he was thinking or feeling, but the tinted lenses of his glasses always obscured that view. I still cannot describe the color of my father's eyes.

That day as I stood before the circular rack of colorful swimsuit choices, I was paralyzed. As usual, I couldn't see my father's eyes, but I felt his impatience and awkwardness like a shroud. Impulsively, I grabbed a suit off the carousel rack—a bland two-piece the color of an eggplant—and trudged into the dressing room. I changed and then stood there, frozen, until my father's booming voice beckoned me.

To have him size me up in that suit, assess my choice, and perhaps even question it was almost too much to take. I hated the suit but couldn't bring myself to say so.

Luckily, he must have felt my anxiety. "Does it fit?" he asked kindly.

"Yes," I whimpered.

I disliked shopping with my father but had no complaints about receiving gifts from him. Those moments were rare but memorable. One time, it was a pale green cardigan sweater that was presented in a clear, plastic wrapper. I opened the plastic, took the sweater out, and held it up so it could unfold. Its buttons had the word *Bayer* etched into their surface, and for some reason this delighted me. It made me think of the aspirin.

Another day my father returned home from work with a white shoe box that looked slightly battered. My mother presented it to me, saying, "Here, try these on." I took the box in my hands and placed it on the floor. Then, dropping down on one knee like a knight, I lifted the slightly torn lid. Inside was the most beautiful pair of shoes I had ever seen: sky blue suede, open-toed wedgies with an ankle strap and a silver buckle. I immediately knew that the shoes hadn't been meant for me at all. Who would buy a pair of shoes like that for an eleven-year-old? They were probably for my mother but the wrong size. I didn't dare question; I only wanted to get them on my feet.

I lifted one shoe from the box as if it were a small, delicate bird, and brushed my hand along the nap of the suede. I kicked off my slippers, so I could quickly try them on. I had difficulty fastening the straps, and my father helped me.

Of course, they were too big but only slightly. I wobbled around for a moment before my mother, with a sigh, declared them "not my size."

"I'll grow into them," I insisted, trying to convince my mother that they had to be mine. "Please, don't give them to anyone else," I begged.

She didn't. She put them on the floor of her closet, where they would be kept safely for me. In the months that followed, I tried those shoes on at least once a week. Finally, almost a full year later, they fit. I fastened the delicate strap over my skinny ponylike ankles and practiced walking around my mother's bedroom.

I studied my feet and my legs in the mirror that was affixed to the back of the bedroom door. I was in love with those shoes and in love with myself wearing them. They were the most exquisite items of clothing I had ever seen. For an entire summer I paraded up and down Locust Avenue teetering on the high wedgies. I climbed telephone poles in them. I shielded them from splashes of the swimming pool's chlorinated water. And I tucked them back into their box every evening.

It was in the mid-1970s that I entered junior high school, and for me the lure of recognizable name brands was just beginning.

I was under the spell of Huckapoo shirts and marshmallows, those horribly clunky shoes with the spongy white soles. I paired my caramel-colored marshmallows with a pair of blue Dickies men's work pants and a stretch terry-cloth polo shirt with short sleeves and a striped collar. I longed to own a pair of lofty platform sandals from Goody Two Shoes.

When a Landlubber jeans shop opened just around the corner from Egbert Junior High, in New Dorp, Staten Island, I was one of the first to rush over and stand, awestruck, in front of the shop's floor-to-ceiling wall display. I had never seen jeans presented that way before, and I remember being amused as I watched the salesgirl mount a tall, wheeled ladder, like the ones used in a library, to retrieve pairs of jeans from the highest shelf. Every pair of jeans was five dollars, and I had begged my mother to give me ten dollars so I could buy two pairs. My new jeans replaced the Dickies, and a pair of leather loafer wedgies replaced the marshmallows.

And then I discovered boys and makeup and shoplifting.

The summer before high school, I began to steal. It was a summer marked by listlessness and boredom as well as anxiety. High school seemed daunting and scary, and in order to relieve some of this tension, my girlfriend Lori and I began to spend time around the local pool hall. There, we befriended a group of equally listless and anxious teenage boys, one of whom—a shy, skinny boy named Gino—became my first boyfriend. We fell into "couple" status in a typically lazy, adolescent way: one night Gino put his arm around me as we walked toward the movie theater, and from that moment on, we were a pair.

Gino and I spent a lot of time at the pool hall, and he taught me how to play eight-ball. When I grew tired of that, he began to teach me how to shoplift. It started with record albums—Elton John, Pink Floyd's *Wish You Were Here*—but quickly progressed to small cosmetic items like Love's Baby Soft body spray and Lip Smacker lip gloss. Inevitably, it extended to clothing.

Garber's was an expensive department store in town, a family-owned place, and that was where I found myself hankering to steal. Garber's had exquisite clothing and the best shoe department; the seats were plush and the salesmen wore suit jackets. My mother shopped there on occasion but not very often.

The first thing I lifted from Garber's was a red shirt with a row of mother-of-pearl buttons and short puffed sleeves. Grabbing the shirt from the hanger, I stuffed it into the front of my denim jacket and bolted, propelled by a rush of adrenaline, out the store's back exit. I ran through the parking lot, past the Pizza Clown restaurant, and up to the boulevard, my heart beating like a jackrabbit's. I double-checked to be sure that the shirt was still in my jacket, tucked close to my chest, as if it were a precious, delicate kitten.

Later my mother noticed the shirt and asked where it came from. I told her it was a gift from my friend Lori.

But my shoplifting career came to an abrupt end on an early-winter day when I tried to steal several pairs of jeans in one go. It was my friend Lori who egged me on. "It's easy," she said. "You just take as many pairs as possible into the dressing room, put on two pairs, then your own jeans over them. Before anyone knows what's missing, you'll be out the door."

It sounded simple, but I should have known better. I didn't have the confidence of a criminal. I followed her instructions but was collared as I walked awkwardly toward the back exit. The store manager decided to call the police. The police in turn summoned my mother.

My mother showed up at the store looking frazzled and concerned rather than angry, and this stabbed right through me. I never imagined that she wouldn't be angry. I almost would have preferred to see her angry. But there she was, oozing love and thoughtfulness. There she was, wearing her cheap rabbit-fur chubby jacket, the one pieced together from different-colored scraps, like a calico cat.

Her hair was wrapped in a turban, and she wore bright red lipstick that amplified the paleness of her skin. She was regal and elegant, and she looked younger than her years. In fact, she was beautiful. But it was the coat that caught my eye. In my rebellious adolescent mind, that cheap fur coat telegraphed an entire world of information. Already I was acutely aware of the status messages relayed by clothing. My mother's coat only seemed to bring attention to the fact that she couldn't afford a proper fur coat. In my fourteen-year-old mind, this was something to be ashamed of.

In that split second, I saw the entire tunnel of her existence come into view. Her past seemed to stretch right into my future. In that moment, I realized that I wanted to be exactly like my mother and nothing like my mother. And this confused me. I just sat there, numb.

I sat there surrounded by the swanky sales staff of Garber's who wore smug smiles and fancy collar brooches. I sat there surrounded by the weary police officers who, with heads bowed, scribbled into their notepads. And there was my mother in her fur chubby — even the name made me cringe — bell-bottom jeans, and high-heeled boots.

I wanted to explain myself. I wanted to explain why I had been shoplifting. I wanted to explain how confused I was about life, boys, love, fear, desire. How confused I was by my own burgeoning yet ill-defined identity. But any words I may have wanted to speak that day just hung in the back of my throat. I watched my mother sign the police officer's notepad, and his nod indicating that she could take me home.

After that I never shoplifted again.

Instead, I ran away from home.

I ran away with Gino, who somehow convinced me that this act of rebellion would help me resolve my confusion. We hid in the shell of a furniture store that was being built on Hylan Boulevard, just down the street from where I lived.

We perched ourselves on a steel girder, and I allowed him to kiss me. I wondered where the limits were. Where did I start? Where did I end? I didn't know. My own questions felt out of the scope of what I could deal with.

♦

Gino and I stayed at the construction site all night. In the morning, I climbed down from the girder and walked up the street to my house, arriving at the back porch like a stray dog.

My mother was one of the easiest people in the world to speak to. She was a good listener, nonjudgmental and wise. She always had helpful advice and dispensed it generously. Friends, both mine and my brothers', spent inordinate amounts of time hanging around our house. They liked the easy atmosphere, and they often confided in her.

Still, I didn't feel I could go to my mother with my own adolescent confusions. After all, she was *my* mother, and my muddled emotions — *I want to be exactly like my mother, and nothing like my mother* — hampered my ability to relate to her with such ease. I knew my behavior was hurting my parents, and I didn't want to continue doing that. Eager to cope with my troubled teenage self, I asked my parents to put me in therapy. They agreed.

The next thing I knew, we were traveling twice a week to a nondescript apartment, where a homely middle-aged woman prodded me about my recent behavior. Her voice bothered me. She spoke too softly, and I would have to ask her to speak up. Her questions annoyed me; I was skeptical of their relevance. And I remember feeling superior to her because I was blond and long limbed, never realizing that this attitude would not help me feel better or make progress. I was the one who was in therapy. I was the one who couldn't handle life. After a short time, I declared myself cured, and therapy came to an end.

I latched on to fashion. I felt that through fashion I could turn fantasy into reality; things could be put in order. I concocted my own rituals for constructing an identity. I began to carry a copy of the book *Cheap Chic,* a paperback filled with images and advice on personal style and places to shop. I carried that book around the way some people carry the Bible. Today, it sits on my bookshelf with dog-eared pages and coffee stains on the cover.

Relaxing in a lounge chair on the back lawn of our modest suburban house, I flipped through the pages of my mother's *Vogue, Cosmopolitan,* and *Glamour* magazines, and I created versions of myself based on the glossy images before me. I dissected the photographs, absorbed and ingested what I saw in them. I knew the names of all the top models: Janice, Gia, Yasmin, and Kelly.

I memorized the names of the photographers and the style of their images: Helmut Newton's photographs were enigmatic tableaux; Francesco Scavullo's were almost gaudily glamorous. Arthur Elgort's were always big smiles, high energy, and wholesomeness; and Richard Avedon's, with their technical precision and white backdrops, struck me as a kind of magical photographic distillation, a blotting out of superficial details that left the essence of the model and what she was wearing intact.

I let these images imprint their messages on me even though I only understood subconsciously what those messages could be.

But there I was, at fifteen, forming the foundation for what would become my career. I would become a fashion editor and writer and eventually a critic of fashion photography and would maintain an almost encyclopedic knowledge of certain fashion photographs.

Did I become addicted to fashion photographs before I became addicted to shopping? Even today, when I look at fashion photographs, I can find them ludicrous, outrageous, and unrealistic. Yet I still feel compelled to dissect and explain them, analyze and understand them. I am drawn to their multilayered messages and remain at their mercy. And as much as I have come to terms with the impact they have had on my life, I still find myself shelling out close to twenty bucks for the latest edition of *Vogue Italia*. For a long time, I remained a slave to such images, forever measuring myself against the idealized self they represent.

At fifteen, the back-to-school girl in me patiently awaited the arrival of the September *Vogue*, always fat as a doorstop, a how-to guide to work out the details of my personal transformation. Whenever my mother returned from shopping with a new magazine, I ferreted it out from the bottom of the grocery bag and immediately claimed it.

Sunday mornings were devoted to my walk to the deli by the train station (no matter the weather) to purchase a copy of the *New York Times*. I wasn't interested in the headlines; I wanted to see the newest fashion advertisements. I was especially anxious to open the *New York Times Magazine* and scrutinize the latest advertisements for designer Betsey Johnson's Manhattan boutique, Betsey Bunky Nini. I would dream of the day when I could shop at Betsey Bunky Nini, and I began to fantasize about becoming a fashion designer myself.

But before I was old enough to travel to Manhattan on my own, I appeased myself with shopping trips to the Staten Island Mall.

The mall had opened in 1973, anchored by Macy's on one end, Sears on the other. Right away, it was steeped in controversy. Islanders were concerned that the mall would kill off many of the mom-and-pop-type businesses in the area. They were right; it did. However, the mall offered something that no mom-and-pop shop could: sanctuary. The large white monolith held within its walls all the comforts of artificiality: plants that neither grew nor wilted; lighting that was neither too strong nor too weak; a perfectly controlled climate. Outside was, quite literally, the wasteland: the Fresh Kills Landfill, one of the world's largest refuse depositories, was just across the road and perpetually animated by the cries of circling seagulls.

Inside the mall, there were thousands of square feet worth of new things to buy. Row upon row of retail therapy. It was at the mall that I purchased my silver Lurex T-shirt, my circle skirt with the Hawaiian floral print, and my first pair of Charles Jourdan shoes. It was at the mall that I struck up my first conversations with sales help, became known for my "good taste," and was encouraged to buy, buy, buy.

♦

In high school, my obsession with fashion reached a new level. Instead of friends, I had my wardrobe. There was my tobacco-colored faux-leather jacket with the fake tortoise-shell buttons and my seersucker striped cowboy shirt with the snap breast pockets. I quit running track in favor of sitting out gym class in the bleachers dressed in my wool herringbone-tweed three-piece "gangster" suit and my spectator pumps with the skinny, stacked heels. I chose ornamentation, dressing up, over exploring the power and strength I might have discovered while playing sports. My exasperated gym teacher warned that she would have to give me a failing grade if I didn't change into my gym shorts and participate in class at least once.

I acquiesced, but only because there was nothing I wanted more than to graduate from high school and get a job. Until that day arrived, I pacified myself with trips to the mall and to lower Manhattan, where I had discovered the discount clothing store Syms.

By the time I graduated from Tottenville High School, the week I turned seventeen, I had already secured a full-time job as a receptionist at a local hair salon. The salon was called Hollywood Swingers and was owned by a curly-haired man named Fred. Since I hadn't yet worked out the details of what I wanted to do with my life, the receptionist job was an easy, temporary solution. I still had vague dreams about pursuing a career in fashion, maybe attending Parsons School of Design or the Fashion Institute of Technology. What I truly wanted to do, yet never spoke about, was to become a writer. I had kept journals and written short stories since I was in grade school, but a career as a writer seemed as far from a realistic possibility as a trip to the moon. I had no idea where to begin to pursue such a path. In the midst of my uncertainty, working at a salon for a few months didn't look bad. My parents didn't voice any objections. By the time I graduated from high school, they had adopted a very relaxed attitude. They had always been open-minded, liberal thinkers, and now their simple mantra seemed to be "whatever makes you happy." They didn't expect much from me, except they hoped that at some point I'd get married and start a family. Essentially, I was free to make my own mistakes.

It didn't matter that the receptionist position in the busy salon would require me to work late on Friday nights and all day Saturdays, preventing me from spending time with friends. It seemed like a small price to pay for finally having my own cash to spend. The job proved to be grueling and hectic. The owner, curly-haired Fred, was demanding and catty and often accused me of "messing up" the appointment book. The intense smell of hair dyes and chemicals started to make me feel ill. Friday evenings, I had to close the salon and balance the books, a task that sometimes became an excruciating ordeal if receipts, expenditures, and the cash in the drawer did not match. I often found myself working until midnight, only to have to return on Saturday morning at 9 a.m. By Saturday evening, I was a complete wreck.

But Sundays and Mondays were my days off. On Sunday, I would buy my copy of the *New York Times*. On Monday, I would be on the express bus to Manhattan so I could shop for things I saw advertised in the newspaper. Often, I would invite my mother to come on my Monday shopping excursions.

In "Shopping," a short story by the writer Joyce Carol Oates, the strained relationship between a mother and a daughter is explored against the backdrop of a trip to the mall. The story opens with Oates describing what had once been the "ritual" Saturday morning shopping trips of Nola and Mrs. Dietrich. It goes on to depict the psychological tug-of-war between a mother who doesn't want to let go of her little girl and a young woman who desperately wants to grow up.

When I was eighteen, I came to understand this ritual of shopping with my mother. I myself realized how the mall could become the perfect backdrop against which the emotional challenges of a young girl about to become a woman might play out. My own advancement toward womanhood began at the mall and then moved to Bloomingdale's, Lord & Taylor, and Syms in downtown Manhattan.

My Monday shopping excursions became as much about leaving my adolescent troubles behind and exploring my independence as they were about purchasing the latest pair of jeans. In the process of coming to recognize myself as a young woman, no longer a troubled teen, I also came to recognize my mother.

Our shopping trips often culminated in lunch somewhere or afternoon tea; tea at the Plaza Hotel was my mother's favorite. If any moments from that time are the most precious, it would be those spent having tea at the Plaza. It was then that I felt I was beginning to break through her invisible barrier, that part of my mother that always seemed hidden. It was in those moments that I got to know more about her: how extremely well-read she was, her great capacity for empathy, her ability to listen, and her wit.

But what I also realized was this: my mother wasn't prepared for my life. Although she had marched in National Organization for Women rallies, kept a copy of *Our Bodies, Ourselves* on prominent display in her bedroom bookcase, and had volunteered at Planned Parenthood, she, like so many women of her generation, was incapable of fathoming exactly how to prepare me to weather the storm of mixed signals that would confront me in the coming decades.

◆ ◆ ◆

And then there was Studio 54 and designer jeans.

By the end of the decade, I had discovered a new group of friends who were as eager to get away from the confines of Staten Island as I was: my boyfriend, Albert; his friends Glen and Angel; and Glen's girlfriend, Anne. Albert was a fledgling fashion photographer, and Angel a musician. Anne, who was slightly older, was already an established hairstylist whose wealthy father had purchased her a salon of her own. Glen, also a hairstylist, was on his way to an apprenticeship at Vidal Sassoon on Fifth Avenue. We were all preoccupied with appearance, style, and fashion. We would drive into

Manhattan, two or three nights a week, to go dancing at Studio 54 and Xenon.

I would dress meticulously for these occasions, with a spirit and energy that I didn't have for anything else in my life. In the car, I would have butterflies just thinking about standing before the intimidating red velvet rope and being singled out from the crowd. As it turned out, the eagle-eyed doorman, Mark, took a liking to our entourage. He found us in the huddle, pointed his godlike finger—*Yes, them. All five*—and we would be ushered in. One night, I wore my new Gloria Vanderbilt corduroy jeans with a purple V-neck sweater, cowboy boots, and a large feather boa around my neck. As we made our way through the gauntlet, a photographer tried to take my picture. As the flash popped, I raised my hand in front of my face, adopted the "no photos" pose that celebrities used, and quickly moved out of his sight. Once inside the cavernous club, Albert and I fell into a fit of giggles. "Where did you learn to do that?" Albert asked. I answered, "I don't know." But I did know exactly where I had learned that pose: in the pages of my fashion magazines. And there were other poses, other personae I knew as well.

Another moment that captivated me: the first time I saw Brooke Shields in her Calvin Klein jeans commercials. I was in the living room with my parents when the image came on the television screen. I recognized the white backdrop and the contorted pose. This was the distilled beauty of the photographer Richard Avedon's fashion photography, only animated. There was Brooke, her head cocked awkwardly as if she had been placed inside a box and her head was hitting the lid. Her legs were awkward too. She looked like she wanted to stretch them, but they were confined by the frame of the television screen.

She spoke: "You want to know what comes between me and my Calvins? Nothing."

"What does she mean by that?" I blurted.

"She means she's not wearing any underwear," my father responded.

I was mesmerized by those ads. I went shopping for my Calvin Klein jeans, and I wore them to Studio 54.

It was at Studio 54 that I met Masao Miyamoto, a Japanese psychiatrist, practicing in New York, who would become my mentor and introduce me to sushi, Kurosawa films, fine French restaurants, and other trappings of a luxurious life-style. It was at his apartment that I first saw a real Andy Warhol painting and a pair of Bose speakers. It was at his apartment that I first used a coffee grinder and saw the sky-line of Manhattan from the windows of a luxury high-rise.

He lived in a building on the east side of midtown Man-hattan at 66th Street. There was a spectacular view and a marble bathroom. Later, I would live in a luxury apartment in Manhattan much like this one, though it would be a long time before the similarity struck me. Down to the floor-boards, the window shades, and the marble bathroom, the places were identical.

Masao wore Versace leather jackets and drove a Porsche,

and he dined at the most exclusive New York restaurants. Once, he invited me to the exquisite French restaurant Lutéce. I had to borrow an evening dress to wear because I owned nothing appropriate. Other times, we simply went to movies or spent time in bookstores or walking in Central Park.

In retrospect, it was an intensely peculiar relationship. It was never sexual and did not involve feelings of romantic love. I have to believe that Dr. Miyamoto and I had a mutual respect and admiration for each other. He always asked for my thoughts and observations, and he enjoyed listening to me express them. We often discussed films and the behavior of characters in them, and one time, after he had redecorated his apartment, he asked me to guess what changes he had made. I guessed that he had taken the Warhol, a Marilyn Monroe silk screen, off the wall. I also guessed that he had sold his imposing loudspeakers and that he probably retired his red leather jacket.

"All correct," he said with great delight. He was thrilled that I was able to discern those things.

I was thrilled too.

When he invited me to participate in his Sunday night dinners, I was both elated and frightened. At these dinners, students from the class he taught at Cornell Medical University gathered to discuss issues related to psychiatry and the arts.

But it was also at those dinners that I got my first taste of the inferiority complex that would haunt me most of my life. I didn't feel I was on the same level as these students, and I wasn't. I had no academic credentials, no higher education.

I found myself playing academic catch-up. I tried to get my hands on all the texts mentioned at the dinners and started reading voraciously. It was through this learning experience with Masao that I solidified my resolve to become a writer.

"You'll live in a fantasy world," was his reply when I told him this. "All writers live in fantasy worlds."

But I was already living in a fantasy world.

I realized I would have preferred to go to university rather than work in a hair salon. I was passionate to learn, and I felt that this revelation was arriving too late. My choice had been a terrific mistake. I had sold myself short. This folly was already hardening around me like a mold. The impossibility of realizing my potential felt like a heavy weight around my neck, and I was confused by all my conflicting desires—I wanted it all and didn't know how to get any of it.

I fell into a depression. One day I found myself unable to get out of bed. I was sleeping for far too many hours in a day. Again, I asked my parents for help. I would need my father's medical insurance to pay for the therapy that I felt I desperately needed. Dr. Miyamoto suggested a colleague of his, Dr. Fisher on 86th Street, and so, for a while, my life revolved around my twice weekly appointments with Dr. Fisher. Nothing more.

Again, as with my first experience with therapy, I found myself impatient with the process. In retrospect, I realize that

I didn't enjoy dismantling my emotional obstacles. I wanted to simply kick them out of the way. This impatience was prompted at moments when therapy seemed to reach into parts of me I wasn't yet ready to see. I cannot say with any accuracy what those moments were, only that they made me uncomfortable. And, as with my first experience with therapy, one day I declared myself better and ended my sessions.

The last time I saw Masao, shortly before he left New York to return to Japan, we had dinner at a restaurant not far from his apartment on the east side. I wore a peculiar outfit, a pair of skintight ultrasuede jeans with a vintage suede Wild West–style fringed jacket, which made me look like a cross between a rocker and Annie Oakley. I was in costume, searching for some new definition of myself. Masao looked at me disapprovingly.

Over dinner, Masao told me about his former secretary. She had become his girlfriend, and she was enjoying the benefits of her new appointment. "She realizes that to be with me means she gets to shop at places like Giorgio Armani, and she is willing to accept that," he explained.

"You mean she is willing to accept that she can be bought," I replied.

He laughed.

I secretly wondered what it might feel like to be bought like that.

Three

CHARGED UP

꘎

My first charge card was a slender wafer of plastic the color of a plum. It was from Macy's, and I received it when I took a part-time job at the Monet jewelry counter on the store's bustling ground floor.

I was twenty years old and still living at home with my parents. The Monet job was a perfect way to earn a little cash while I tried to get my modeling career launched. I had been accepted on the "test board" at the Ford Modeling Agency, which meant that I had the privilege of spending countless hours running around Manhattan visiting various photographers' studios. There, I could present photos of myself with the hope that these photographers, having seen me in person, would be interested in taking even more photos of me. I would get to use these photos in my "book," which I would then lug around to potential clients in my quest for paid modeling work.

I was gleeful knowing that with my new credit card I

could purchase clothing, wear it for my photo shoots, and return it the next day. This was common practice in the modeling world, and I took to it like a pro. As long as the price tags were still intact and the clothing wasn't damaged, returns were accepted, no questions asked.

There was nothing I liked better than shopping, and the idea that I could shop perpetually, via my new plastic card and Macy's liberal return policy, made me euphoric. The only problem with this scenario was that, more often than not, I wanted to keep the clothes I had purchased. At some point, this buy-and-return scenario had reached its credible limit for me; I was more interested in earning enough money to actually buy and keep things rather than let them go. Still, I was an ideal credit card customer: I diligently made my minimum payment each month and continued to buy to my maximum credit limit.

Eventually, I landed my first big modeling job: a full day's work for the stupefying rate of $1,200 a day, roughly the same amount my father made in a week. "Here it is," I said joyfully, as I presented my check to be deposited into my new checking account. My father looked at the rectangular piece of paper as if it were a message from another planet. He was silent.

"You made that much in one day?" my brother Francis chimed in.

I could feel something inside me tighten as this scene

played out. It felt as if a fishing line had been looped around my heart. The guilt I felt about that paycheck stayed with me, lodging itself in my psyche and running interference with my desire to earn money to possess worldly goods. Many years later, I would share this story with friends on different occasions, as if in the act of retelling it I would be enlightened. I never was.

As things turned out, I hardly ever earned that kind of day rate again. My modeling career sputtered along with small, occasional jobs. My father found a tiny studio apartment for me in Manhattan, and I moved in. In order to pay my rent, I had to supplement my income with part-time jobs. I took jobs as a receptionist at a health club, and then as a hostess at a restaurant, and then I would work the coat check at swanky uptown restaurants.

When spring arrived and the coat check business dried up, I was forced to find other sources of income. It was my friend Kim, a blond Sharon Stone look-alike, already divorced from a famous baseball player before she reached her mid-twenties, who told me about the flight attendant recruitment interview. "Do you want to come?" she said, as she sucked on a cigarette dramatically, like a movie star. I imagined that anywhere she went, there must be some element of glamour. So I said yes.

One rainy Saturday we drove out to JFK Airport in her Honda NSX, and we sat in a windowless room taking a test.

By the end of the day, we were both recruited and due to fly to Florida the following week for our training session.

A few weeks after that, I was in the air working a flight to London.

It's not surprising that I thought of my career as a flight attendant as an extended shopping trip. As soon as I landed in London, I headed for Kings Road. There, after spending hours hopping in and out of trendy boutiques, I finally settled in a vintage clothing store where I bought a men's linen suit. The suit was the color of butter, the linen starched to attention. On the jacket's inside pocket, a label read: "custom tailored by King's Tailors for Mr. Long."

The following week, on a flight to Paris, I discovered the boutiques in Saint-Germain, but they proved to be too expensive. I ended up shopping in the more popular Les Halles and returned home with a pair of red patent leather high-heeled pumps and a cheap satin cheongsam. In my first few weeks as a flight attendant, I nearly spent more money than I earned but eventually was able to rein things in. Later that summer, when I was scheduled on a daily turnaround to San Juan, Puerto Rico, there were no layovers, no shopping, and it occurred to me that I had another rather exhausting and tedious job.

◆ ◆ ◆

In the mideighties, I began to realize that my job as a flight attendant was not a stepping-stone to bigger and better things.

After being laid off from my job, I became depressed and despondent. This would be the second time in my adult life I would succumb to depression. My woes were precipitated by what appeared to be a lack of options. I applied for several flight attendant jobs, none of which panned out, then attempted, unsuccessfully, to resurrect my modeling career. I ended up taking part-time work at a talent agency. I had pretty much given up on the idea of becoming a writer, a magazine journalist, even though that is what I knew I wanted more than ever.

I was approaching my midtwenties, and feeling that nothing was gelling in a significant way. Not only was my career nonexistent, my romantic life was also in shambles. In Paris, I had fallen in love, but the impossibilities of a long-distance romance kept the relationship from developing and only added to my feelings of desperation.

I latched on to a photographer back in New York who dazzled me with his Midtown loft and exotic past.

His name was Marius, and over a pasta dinner at his place, he regaled me with stories of his adventures in Central America as a photojournalist. He was rugged and handsome and mature. He was much older than me and appeared to have his life in order. I was smitten and after a few weeks found myself subletting my tiny studio apartment and moving into his spacious loft.

Within a few months, things seemed serious enough to warrant an engagement, a ring, and a party. In hindsight, it's clear that the relationship progressed much too fast, but this quick-fix method of dealing with difficult moments in life would become my pattern, repeated at several other junctures.

At the engagement party I was more than willing to bask in the promise of the event—marriage, the fairy-tale ending—and forget about the fact that I barely knew the man who I was now calling my fiancé.

My most vivid memory of that party is what I wore: a pair of black suede trousers and a white silk shirt with billowing pirate sleeves that I had bought at Bloomingdale's. The trousers were the first pair of leather pants I had ever owned, and I can remember walking through the loft trying to get used to the way the heavy leather shifted counter to the movement of my body. Suddenly, there I was, wanting to be like my mother again. I was mimicking the way she pranced around the house in her palazzo pants. I was moving my life in the same trajectory: toward a happy marriage.

Almost immediately after the engagement, the relationship began to sour. Because our relationship was mainly yoked around physical attraction, I found myself becoming jealous and demanding. I didn't like the way he paid attention to other women and found him too gregarious and flirtatious. I also didn't like the way he invited people to show up at the loft at all hours, the way he said, *"Mi casa es su casa"* to total strangers. We began to fight about everything, and finally, one day, it reached a peak with a blowout that left me packing my bags. We called off the engagement.

But a few months later, we were back together and, practically on a whim, I challenged Marius to marry me. Thinking that marriage would solve things and keep me from having to face other difficult parts of life, I plunged into that commitment. Marriage seemed like a solution, the thing that would pin my wings to the velvet cushion.

Besides, marriage was what was expected of me, wasn't it? At least that's what I imagined. In marriage, I thought I could close the lid on a box and take things from there. In marriage, I thought there would be a level of certainty, and an order to life, that I never seemed to be capable of achieving on my own.

So, on September 17, 1987—wearing a cream-colored, short-sleeved wool sweater from Agnès B; a brown pin-check pencil skirt; and pointy-toed, chocolate brown pumps—I was married at City Hall in lower Manhattan. After the ceremony, my new husband, our best man Rodney, a foreign correspondent for *Newsweek* magazine, and I went to lunch.

My husband was sociable and charming, but I also found him to be domineering and volatile, and sometimes possessive. "If you're not with me, you're against me," he stated, in no uncertain terms, as we sat having dinner in our favorite Japanese restaurant.

He went on to explain that this meant I would be required to work as his assistant. He was a photographer. I would help him lug the equipment around, set up the lighting, and make sure everyone on the set was happy. I realized this meant he would be in control of my whereabouts as well as the money I made. My earning power would be directly linked to his.

Despite my strong misgivings, I willingly shackled myself to this arrangement.

"But I want to make a deal with you," I said imploringly as I leaned in toward him. "I want to be able to take writing classes in the evening."

I thought this would be enough to dissolve the lump of doubt that clumped inside me like a hairball, and so I began to reassure myself with this arrangement.

And, of course, I pacified myself with shopping.

After the Macy's card, what seemed like an avalanche of offers for other credit cards came pouring in. They were impossible to resist. It seemed like money was being thrown at me. My credit cards made me feel rich, even though I barely had a penny to my name.

I also had the idea that having credit cards meant I was building a credit history, and that this was a good thing. Those two words —*credit history*— sounded adult. The more cards, the quicker the history. The idea of being able to buy something for $100 but only having to pay back $10 each month for a year was magical. I hardly ever looked at the interest rates or the fine print. Some cards came preapproved and made me question the whole process. How in the world could I be preapproved? Who had approved me?

I filled out the application forms, mailed them in, and waited, as someone waits for a cake to bake. Occasionally, an envelope would arrive in the mail with something rectangular, hard, and plastic in the upper right corner. I liked running my hand over the envelope, feeling the new card, and tearing the paper to discover what the spending limit would be. It was always a mysterious number, as random as a bingo call. There seemed to be no obvious explanation for how my credit limits were determined.

In her book *The Overspent American: Why We Want What We Don't Need,* Juliet Schor refers to this practice of offering credit to people who can barely afford it as "credit pushing."

It made sense: if I was on my way to becoming a shopping addict, a pusher was a necessary accomplice, but this wasn't clear at the time. I, like millions of other naive credit card customers, was completely unaware of financial deregulation practices that were taking place behind the scenes. It was these practices that would help make lending profitable and spawn marketers who were more than willing to take the risk of lending to marginal buyers — students, senior citizens, and those like me with limited incomes.

I accepted my new plastic cards with excitement. I was part of a generation groomed to think nothing of paying on credit, a generation caught up in the whirlwind of instant gratification.

Soon, acquiring credit cards became something of a game, and by the mid-1980s, I had at least four department store credit cards, an American Express of my own, and a gold American Express courtesy of my husband. There was also a Visa and MasterCard somewhere in the mix.

At first, I was a dutiful credit card customer, always paying my minimums on time. I had been raised with this kind of responsible spending and had never known anyone who had trouble with personal debt. Even though I didn't understand much about money, my natural inclination was to be careful with it. In addition, my mother had taken a job as a loan officer, and my father had become president of a credit union.

Although I had several department store credit cards, most of my time was spent at Macy's since it was only a short walk from our Midtown loft. It was at Macy's that I most enjoyed lolling through the designer fashion floors or killing time in the hosiery department. I bought clothing for myself, as I had always done, and skin-care products for my chronically troubled complexion. I also bought overpriced food from the gourmet food hall located in the basement. But I did not spend excessively, carelessly, or beyond my budget. On a lined yellow notepad, I kept tally of how much money I earned and how much I was spending.

I continued in my work arrangement with my husband, but despite the perks — celebrities coming to our loft for photo sessions, occasional work or play trips — I was unhappy with his overbearing personality. We fought more often than not, sometimes boisterously.

Still, after almost a full year of marriage, the decision was made to finally have a church wedding. Again, the earliest notions I had of myself held sway over me: as the only daughter, I felt I owed my parents a proper wedding. I felt I owed it to my father to walk me down the aisle. I also harbored some hope that this missing ingredient, the wedding, would set my tumultuous relationship with Marius on a more even keel.

My gown was vintage, purchased from a small shop in SoHo. The church was on 34th Street. The reception was at a downtown restaurant, a Tribeca boîte with French doors that opened onto a wrought-iron terrace that ran directly over the Franklin Street subway line. The wedding, held on a stunning July day, went off perfectly with extended family and friends, some of whom had known me since I was a child, all in attendance.

There was a long honeymoon in the Caribbean, paid for with the money we had received as wedding gifts. Saving that money would have been the smart thing to do, but we didn't. It was a silly indulgence that included a rented house, on the island of Saint Lucia, that overlooked cocoa fields and had a stunning view of the Pitons. There was a lounge with a cathedral ceiling, a wraparound porch, and a cook who came every day while we were at the beach to prepare sumptuous local dishes. We would arrive at dusk to a pot simmering on the stove.

It was during that trip that I learned to scuba dive, and I fell in love with the sport. I fell in love with the sensation of floating through the water, of hearing the steady rhythm of my own breath underwater. Scuba diving put me in touch again with my physical abilities. I was exhilarated.

At the end of August when we returned from our honeymoon, the word I would use to describe myself would be *whole*. I felt complete in a way that I had not in a long time, but that feeling would be short-lived. The relationship quickly devolved into its usual storminess. Neither of us was happy in the marriage. I felt I had made a mistake but could find no legitimate way of explaining it. Why had I asked so many people to participate in our spectacle of a wedding?

◆ ◆ ◆

The call came out of nowhere, a sucker punch delivered through the receiver of an ordinary phone with an ordinary ring on an ordinary day.

"Your mother's in the hospital," my father said, and then before I had a chance to react, "It's okay; it's not serious. You don't need to come."

"But what is it exactly?"

He explained that she had gone to the emergency room with stomach pains. He and my mother had just finished decorating the Christmas tree when my mother fell ill. At first, she simply lay down, tried to sleep it off. But after a few hours, the pain became excruciating, and my father had to call an ambulance.

"They've stabilized her," my father said. "But they're still not sure what it is. They think it may be her gallbladder. They're running some tests."

Then my father put my mother on the phone, and I immediately burst into tears. I had not wanted to burden her like that, but the tears came anyway. "I'm okay," she said, but she sounded weak.

A few days later, another call came: "She's not doing too well. I think you'd better come."

Things moved quickly: intensive care, false hopes, whispered promises. There were confusing conversations with surgeons, unanswered questions. I sat at the side of her bed; in the waiting room; on the hard, cold chairs in the cafeteria. My husband had an assignment to photograph an actor in Chicago and insisted that I accompany him. We took the train and photographed the cranky, uncooperative celebrity in a ten-minute session, rat-a-tat style, right there in the train station. Then we packed up the gear, boarded a train, and returned home the same evening. I did not want to be traveling; I wanted to be close to my mother.

By the end of the second week, she had been through several operations and various prognoses were offered. It was no longer her gallbladder but her pancreas. There was no clear explanation for what was going wrong. We huddled like football players over discussions on specialists and strategies. Then there was a tracheotomy, a tube in her throat, and a slow intravenous drip.

The last time I saw my mother alive, she was unconscious in her hospital bed. I stood next to her, watching her sleep, unclenched her fists, and left.

♦ ♦ ♦

Early in our marriage, my husband built a closet for me. He sat at the kitchen table working on the design and carefully chose each piece of wood. With his own two hands, he constructed a place for my most precious possessions: my clothing, my shoes, and my jewelry. In the end, it was a magnificent closet—with special little cubicles for stockings and under-wear, and an overhead storage space that was large enough to sleep in. I remember him climbing into that overhead com-partment to show me. Yes, he fit in it; this made me laugh.

After my mother's death, my life continued to fall apart domino style.

I neglected my own need to mourn and grieve and con-centrated on caring for my father. His pain and loss trumped my own. *I can put things on hold,* I told myself, and I did. I sidelined my grief.

But my mother's death propelled me into uncharted ter-ritory. After the shock of death, it's not uncommon for survi-vors to look like they are holding up well. At first, I remember believing that because I could eat, sleep, walk, and talk as I normally had, I was handling things okay.

Yet soon I began to have the strange feeling that even though it was my mother who had died, part of me was now missing. I felt hollowed out by the loss. I needed to beckon my inner strength, but didn't seem to have any. Some critical aspect of me went into hiding. *I am empty,* I remember telling myself.

In a stupor, in a trance, I began to shop away count-less afternoons. Shopping was the one thing that provided respite from this void. Each purchase provided a small mor-sel of pleasure, and that was better than feeling nothing at all. The simple act of buying myself something seemed nec-essary and healing. I can remember feeling fragile, unstable, and almost zombielike, and shopping was the most familiar, normal, and stabilizing activity I could imagine. So I began to shop nearly every day.

I spent countless hours meandering through the designer, junior, and young-contemporary sections of Macy's, Lord & Taylor, and Bloomingdale's. Often, I felt the need to be alone in these shops, losing myself in mazes of overstuffed display racks and metal T-stands.

The shopping environment became as critical for me as the shopping. I deliberately sought out stores that felt isolated and removed from the real world. It quickly became apparent that shops were more than willing to assist me. Blocked-off windows, for example, helped create the illusion of total shopping immersion.

One day, in Macy's, having strayed too far to the fringes of a coat section, I came across an undressed window offering a clear view of 34th Street. I remember being completely unnerved by that experience.

Back at home, my husband started complaining about my grim mood. I tried to hide it from him, which took considerable effort and wore me down. On more than one occasion, I went shopping just to escape his glare.

My marriage was unraveling. There were constant arguments and long spells of not speaking. I finally quit assisting my photographer-husband, and this appeared to be the proverbial last straw. A voice inside me kept saying, *Use this time to gather your strength.* It would manifest itself from time to time in small bursts of action. I knew I would need to find a new source of income, and I still harbored dreams of working at a magazine. So I mustered the energy to write a letter to Grace Mirabella, former editor of *Vogue,* who was looking for staff for her new project, an eponymous fashion magazine. My letter yielded an interview with Mirabella herself, which made me ecstatic. But I flubbed the interview. After looking at my résumé, Mirabella had suggested that my modeling background might make me a good candidate for the position of model editor. Instead of agreeing and jumping at the chance, I let my insecurity get in the way. I insisted I wasn't sufficiently qualified for that position, and the interview quickly ended.

In late 1989, with another burst of energy, I sought out a lawyer to file for divorce. On a winter day, I trudged through the slush-filled streets to an office on Park Avenue and then proceeded to sit in front of a highly polished oak desk and spell out the details of my situation to a serious-looking man with a balding head, a blue shirt, and thick-rimmed glasses. It wasn't very complicated, he said: no children involved, no property owned, no great sums of money to divide. He suggested that since I was "still young enough," it would be best to reach an agreement on a cash settlement and simply move on with my life.

This time, I agreed.

By January 1990, a full year after my mother's death, I found myself newly separated, almost penniless, and several thousand dollars in credit card debt. I had just received a check for $4,000 — $500 of which would go to my lawyer — from my soon-to-be-ex husband. He had agreed to this amount as a settlement. I had agreed to sign off on any other financial claims to my husband's assets. He got to stay in our Midtown loft. I got to move back to my old shoebox-size studio apartment with paper-thin walls, which I had sublet during the course of my brief and tumultuous marriage. The only thing left at that point was the mandatory year wait before the final divorce decree could be signed.

Four

WELCOME TO THE NINETIES

⁂

I can still picture myself standing at the departure gate at JFK Airport about to embark on a trip to Europe to meet my new boyfriend, Thomas. I wore my fat, cuddly teddy-bear coat. How innocent it seems: a coat that resembles a stuffed toy. I had purchased it for $600 at Saks Fifth Avenue shortly before my mother died. "I bought this fabulous coat," I remember telling her over the phone.

She asked me to describe it. It had a deep, plush, fake fur pile the color of roasted chestnuts, a row of plastic toggle buttons that were meant to look like real horn, and a large peaked hood. I used to rub my hand up and down the nap of the fur and watch the color change from light to dark.

My husband had boiled over when I came home with that coat. This was an extravagance that was "not in our budget," he barked. I hadn't bought myself a good winter coat in years, and I calculated this one as a worthy investment. I explained that if I wore it for at least three years, the coat would end up costing $200 per year, and more years would yield an even better return. Normally I would have buckled under my husband's rage, but something spurred me on. I resisted his anger and kept the coat.

So there I was, almost a full year after that purchase, sitting in a molded plastic chair at Gate 18, waiting to board my flight. The coat felt like a godsend. It provided padding, warmth, and comfort when everything ahead of me seemed murky and uncertain. I had no idea what I would do next, how I would survive. Yet in my luggage were two new pairs of shoes, suede flats. I had bought them at Macy's in pretty much the same way I had started to buy many things over those months when I saw my marriage coming to an end: recklessly. I had bought elbow-length leather gloves and pair after pair of printed tights. I bought an Yves Saint Laurent denim skirt on sale that was so severely cut in a pencil-point shape it forced me to hobble. I bought an off-white wool sweater that tied, like a kerchief, at the waist. I still own it but almost never wear it. I bought riding pants. I was forever buying riding clothes, although I've never been on a horse in my life. And even though my steady income working as my husband's assistant had just about dried up by that time, I had continued to shop.

And so there I was on the plane, and buying, in the same reckless manner, a bottle of Coco perfume from the duty-free trolley. Just another extravagance that I felt I needed: a new decade, a new lover, and a new perfume.

♦

That trip marked the beginning of a relationship that would end up lasting the entire decade. It also marked my introduction into both a life and a shopping style that I would find myself seduced by. At the time, this all appeared to be a stroke of outrageous fortune. I was barely out of my marriage and already embarking on a new relationship that appeared to hold so much promise.

The relationship was with Thomas, a German entrepreneur, who had recently moved to New York and set up a lucrative business. He had an intimidating gray-eyed gaze and a thick German accent, and I remember being amused by the way he always said *"mein Gott"* about anything that surprised him.

He had been an acquaintance of my husband's and mine for almost a year, and when my marriage was unraveling, he had talked me through some of the turbulent moments. His advice was always reasoned and rational, and above all, he mothered me. The mothering is what felt right and perhaps what I was most attracted to.

Thomas had invited me to join him on a trip to Europe, the very week I was moving back into my old studio apartment, and I jumped at the chance. The thought of spending time alone in that dark, tiny apartment was daunting—the opportunity to avoid it infinitely more appealing. There was my pattern of avoidance, once again.

♦

By the time my flight landed, and I stepped off the plane in Milan, I was worse for wear: bleary-eyed, with a large pimple on my chin. And I must have looked frightening because I can remember Thomas saying *"mein Gott"* the moment he laid eyes on me. The first days were spent at an apartment that belonged to a friend of Thomas's in Lake Como, but in my mind they will forever remain a blur of rest and recovery: loads of sleep, long chats, and steaming hot cups of tea.

It wasn't until we arrived in Düsseldorf that I began to feel human again. The problems awaiting me back home seemed far away, at least for the moment, and although I felt uncomfortable staying at the home of his parents, he tried to make it easier for me by installing me in the attic apartment that he had inhabited as a teenager. The room was musty with disuse, dark, and filled with relics from his past: a dusty turntable and old LPs, a worn leather sofa. But I remember looking around and feeling surprised and relieved that there was simplicity to the place. It was nothing like his luxurious apartment back in New York. It was clear that his family was not wealthy and that he had been raised in a modest environment; this revelation made me admire him.

His parents, although kind, were skeptical. Who was the not-yet-divorced woman who spoke only English? His mother laid a table of sandwich meats, cheeses, coffee, and cakes. His father tried out a few words in English. It was clear that they missed their only son, his absences and reappearances important markers in their lives. My presence seemed an obstacle. The constant translation made the conversation bumpy and unnatural.

In order to ease the tension, Thomas whisked me off to the center of town to get a taste of Düsseldorf and do some shopping. It turned out that Thomas probably liked shopping even more than I did, but for distinctly different reasons. It was then, during the remainder of the trip, that I got my first sense of Thomas's level of shopping.

Königsallee could be described as the Düsseldorf version of Fifth Avenue. My first impression: a cliché of expensive sports cars and women in furs. As soon as we parked the car and stepped onto the sidewalk, I felt insecure. My teddy-bear coat seemed sorely out of place.

When we stopped off at a trendy boutique called Eickhoff, my discomfort spiked. The place buzzed with young sales clerks who were all very tall, attractive, and perfectly groomed. I had been used to my trips to Macy's, where I would stroll around alone for hours, searching for something to buy. The beaming lights and buzz of the boutique almost made me dizzy. When I took a sip from the glass of champagne that appeared in my hand, I felt giddy. I waltzed about the store and tried to be nonchalant to mask my insecurity. I found myself looking at a dark blue suit.

"Try it on," said Thomas.

I stumbled on my reply. "No, really. I . . . no, it's okay."

But he insisted, and the next thing I knew I found myself

in a large dressing room with my champagne settled on a small glass table, and several pairs of high-heeled pumps, in a variety of sizes, lined up on the carpet.

In the relative silence of the dressing cabin, I examined the suit that hung from a small brushed metal knob. It was an extraordinary suit: dark blue lightweight gabardine wool. I pondered the situation I found myself in: there I was, barely out of my marriage, standing in a boutique in Düsseldorf sipping champagne and being asked by a man I hardly knew to try on a Jean Paul Gaultier suit.

I looked at the suit again. It had pegged trousers and a double-breasted jacket with a quirky detail: a slash under each armpit. The idea was to wear a white shirt beneath the dark suit so that flashes of white could peek through. The savvy salesgirl had placed a white shirt in the dressing room as well, so I could experience the full effect of this sartorial trick.

I had heard of the Paris-based designer Jean Paul Gaultier and had seen some of his creations in shops, but this was fresh off the runway, and I had never been able to afford such extravagances. Any designer labels I had purchased came from outlets or were old stock.

I looked at the price tag. The suit was labeled at several thousand deutsche marks, which was the equivalent of roughly $1,200. With only my $3,500 settlement in my bank account, I was in no position to buy such a suit, let alone allow the intimacy of its touching my naked skin. In addition, I didn't know Thomas well enough to discern whether he was trying to ply me with presents. I would try on the suit, just to be polite, and leave it at that.

The moment I fastened the last button of the snug-fitting jacket, I felt changed. The tailoring was impeccable, detailed, and precise. The jacket exaggerated my shoulders slightly but not too much, and the darts created the illusion of an hourglass waist. The pants had a crease like a knife, as well as a hidden watch pocket. They were the perfect length, and I wished they weren't. I would have disliked myself in the suit if something had been wrong, but there wasn't. Everything was perfect.

I held up my arms to expose the quirky armpit detail and laughed. It was the most fabulous suit I had ever worn!

I emerged from the cabin wearing the suit, the white shirt, and a pair of the high-heeled pumps that had been provided. I stood in front of the three-way mirror. Despite my bad complexion, my skin-and-bones frame, I looked remarkably fresh, alive. And when I stood before the mirror, I realized that the "me" staring back had completely obliterated the "me" who had walked into the boutique a few minutes earlier.

I was familiar with the transformative powers of clothing from having worked as a model. The whole process of making a fashion photograph—the hair, makeup, location, and clothes—revolves around creating an illusion. Arriving at a photo studio for a shoot carries the expectation of becoming someone else. That's part of the job. Still, I had never felt so transformed by a garment as I did that day in the Jean

Paul Gaultier suit. Surveying myself, I was overcome with the feeling that the suit had uncovered some aspect of me that had always been hidden.

"You look super," Thomas said. He smiled and touched my hair. The saleswoman who had been helping us handed me a fresh glass of champagne and instructed me to stroll around in the suit for a few minutes. "Get used to yourself," she said.

Get used to myself.

There was no need for that. I was already seduced. All reason had gone out the window; my sense of reality was left somewhere in the heap of clothing that lay on the dressing room floor. I wanted to have that suit and had already decided I would buy it for myself.

I told the sales associate that I would take it. Thomas looked at me, startled. He was not aware of my financial situation, but he knew enough about what was going on in my life to know it wasn't fantastic. Over the days we spent together, we had spoken about many things, but I had not confided the details of my financial situation. He knew about my life before, knew my ex-husband, and had been to our loft, so he had some idea of our lifestyle. And like most of my friends, he had watched my marriage unravel and knew that I had to move back to my tiny studio apartment. He wasn't stupid, and he was aware that a suit at that price was probably something I could not afford.

As I took my American Express card from my wallet, he pushed it aside. "No, don't do that," he said. He presented his credit card instead. "Let me buy this as a gift for you."

♦ ♦ ♦

A simple purchase, and so many wheels were set in motion.

We returned to New York with my new Jean Paul Gaultier suit. The suit seemed like a mistake in my tiny apartment. It looked monumental next to all the other inferior clothing that I owned. I didn't even own the proper kind of hanger that would hold the shape of the jacket. Thomas had to loan me one of his; it was black lacquered wood with gold-plated hardware. The hanger looked even more conspicuous, foreign, and precious than the garment it was designed to hold.

All this made me look at my existing wardrobe with a critical eye. It was mix-and-match style. There were many separate items that made little sense together. Things had been acquired according to a scatterbrained strategy. I had not, in fact, started building a functional wardrobe, but simply loaded up on whimsical purchases that left me in debt.

This growing debt left me with the gnawing need to tell Thomas about my situation. The next morning, I called him at his office. "Would you just meet me downstairs?" I said. "Just for a few minutes. I need to talk to you." I walked from my place on 29th Street up to Park and 52nd. When I arrived, Thomas was already standing outside, waiting for me. He looked happy to see me.

It was a beautiful spring day. The sharp sunlight exaggerated the exquisite quality of the suit he wore. The pants hung in folds, the pleated front was so expertly executed.

The jacket, unbuttoned, seemed to have just the right weight and drape. His shoes were freshly polished.

By contrast, my own outfit suddenly looked ridiculous. I was wearing a pair of forest green spandex shorts that stopped just above the knee and a dark green cotton T-shirt with small gathers around the bust. On Park Avenue, amid the hustle and bustle of real people with real jobs, I felt sorely out of place, wearing an outfit more suited for a night-club than the glaring light of day. When I looked down at my feet, I felt even worse: black leather flats with a pointed toe that made my size 9 feet look positively clownlike.

In recalling all these sartorial details, I am reminded that something about me must have already started to change. I was paying attention to external appearances — the drape of a pant leg, the shine on a shoe — as if they had acquired a new relevance or a significance that I had somehow previously failed to observe.

This discomfort with my appearance almost seemed to carry more weight than the problem I had come to address: I owed money on my credit cards and had started to fall behind on payments. I was trying to get work as a photographer's assistant, but that wasn't proving to be as successful as I would have liked. The $3,500 from my divorce settlement was almost gone.

"I'm giving up," I blurted as I approached Thomas. He looked at me with a confused expression. He must have thought I was trying to back out of our burgeoning romantic relationship.

"I mean, I don't know what to do with my life anymore," I continued. "Nothing is what it should be. I have no career. I have no choice but to become a cashier at a supermarket," I rattled on ridiculously.

"Calm down," Thomas said in his reassuringly steady voice. "We'll get everything in order."

He had to get back to work.

Several months later, I moved out of the tiny studio and in with Thomas. The day of the move, there were several things left behind in the old apartment: a set of two crystal champagne glasses, a book of photographs of the Empire State Building, and a faux-fur leopard-print coat I had never worn. The price tag was still attached.

At this time, Thomas started to help me clean up my credit card mess. I had, in total, close to $2,000 in debt, which at the time seemed monumental. He made me get rid of all the department store cards and use whatever money I had to catch up on back payments. Now, living rent-free, I would not have to worry about that monthly expense. However, even with these measures, my credit rating had already suffered damage. It would take years to get my poor payment history off my record and my good credit restored.

Thomas brought a sense of order and control to my life that felt right at that moment. After moving in together, I adapted myself to his way of being. Living in a luxury high-rise forced me to work out new details that went with the lifestyle. Just to come in and out of the building—entering or exiting through the gilded tunnel of a lobby—meant a new way of walking and talking. This was where I said hello to the concierge and tipped the doorman. This was where I allowed someone else to hail me a cab. This is where my Jean Paul Gaultier suit looked right; my teddy-bear coat started to look all wrong. This is where my acquaintance with luxury would prove to be a seductive attraction.

It took me a while to grasp the nuances of this new lifestyle. I couldn't believe my luck to be instantly propelled into a situation that included a Midtown apartment with a Central Park view and shopping trips around the world. We started to travel: Venezuela, Paris, Hamburg, and South Beach, Florida. Everywhere we went, we shopped.

I decided to augment my work as well, giving up the idea of continuing as a photographer's assistant and concentrating on a career as a fashion stylist instead. Setting up camera equipment had never been my dream; that was just a part of my past, a part of my former marriage. It was over. I was trying to be practical. Now I was finally aware that my knowledge of photo shoots and fashion formed a feasible basis for a new career.

I still harbored a desire to write and to work at a magazine, but just getting my life up and running again seemed an insurmountable task. I simply felt enormously lucky that things appeared to be falling into place.

♦ ♦ ♦

Thomas encouraged me to get rid of the many superfluous credit cards that I had amassed during my marriage. He made me narrow them down to my American Express and Visa. I happily obliged.

Yet at that time, I didn't think of myself as having a shopping problem. I simply thought of myself as a young woman who had had a spate of bad luck. I had heard stories about divorces, how they wreaked havoc with finances. That was my story: a divorce, a death, and a financial meltdown.

But what was closer to the truth was this: My mother's death had exacerbated something that had probably been there all along. Was it low self-esteem? Was it unresolved grief? Was it a lack of something that resided in me all that time?

With Thomas, I had the chance to continue hiding from this minefield of questions and from myself. I hid behind what appeared to be a curtain of outrageous fortune. Almost all my friends praised the relationship. What a great stroke of luck for me, everyone had said. *Wow, you met a fantastic guy and moved into a fancy apartment, and he buys you beautiful clothes.* Today, it still fascinates me how few questions were asked about the emotional underpinnings of the whole relationship. But I had masterfully sidelined my grief. Why should anyone have questioned the happiness I displayed? It still perplexes me how unwilling I was to ask myself those questions.

The only person to question the situation was my cousin Joan. One evening at a family dinner at her home in New

Jersey, I rattled on enthusiastically about Thomas, the suit, the trips to Europe, and the apartment that overlooked Central Park. Joan listened carefully, told me how great it all sounded and how she couldn't wait to meet him. Nevertheless, she knew how wounded I was by my mother's death, and she could see past the gleeful veneer.

"Be careful," she said.

"What do you mean?" I asked.

"Give yourself time," she answered.

Those words were true — *give yourself time*. I hadn't given myself time. Even before my mother's death, I had been impatient with myself. I had always wanted to find answers quickly: quit the therapy and fling myself into fashion. Come home from Paris heartbroken and throw myself into marriage. File for divorce and jump into a new relationship before the ink had even dried on my separation agreement.

I reassured Joan that I was all right. I knew what I was doing.

Things tumbled forward from there. Thomas continued to bathe me with attention, and he also started to offer his instruction. He had an opinion about every aspect of my appearance: my clothing, my fingernails (they were not properly maintained), and my teeth, which needed to be straightened.

Once on a trip to Florida, the issue became my denim cutoffs. "They look cheap," Thomas declared, as we sat at the bar of the Delano Hotel, having a drink. Suddenly, I felt cut down, inferior. But when I looked at Thomas, elegant and groomed (he almost never wore jeans), I realized that we weren't exactly a match. He dressed like a sophisticated man while I dressed like a teenager. Still, I put up a fight. "They're a part of who I am," I insisted, feeling, even as the words left my mouth, that I was no longer sure if it was true. When we returned from the trip, I tossed the jeans in the bin. The me of the cut-off denims and the teddy-bear coat was being shown the door.

I began to shop, almost exclusively, with Thomas and allowed him to choose things for me. Most of the time, his taste prevailed. His instructions on what to wear and how to wear it were accepted and adopted.

The next Christmas, we were in Düsseldorf again, spending the holiday with his parents. We would remain at their home for several days, and I would again find myself installed in the attic bedroom. This arrangement was uncomfortable and stifling, but I felt helpless to do anything about it.

We would go shopping at the Königsallee again, but this time I felt different. I had been transformed over that year and now easily took my place among the well-dressed women who flooded the shopping arcades on those gloomy, overcast December afternoons.

One day as we strolled past the jewelry shop Hesterman, Thomas suggested we go in to look at some watches. I recall stepping inside that shop with him and being impressed that the owner sprang up from serving another client to shake Thomas's hand. After introductions, we were led to two straight-backed chairs set in front of a large leather-covered table. The shop owner disappeared behind a lacquered door and emerged a minute later with a small box in his hands.

As the man sat down and started to unwrap the small box, I sensed what was happening. Before I could process the thought completely, Thomas slid the box across the desk's surface, looked at me, and said, "I'd like you to marry me." As he did so, he opened the box to reveal a brilliant diamond surrounded by a thick band of platinum.

Because I had jumped into marriage once with little regard for the realities of the commitment, I was not ready to jump into marriage again. I felt beaten up after my divorce, like a failure. I was still unresolved about my previous motivations and mistakes and unresolved in my grief. Marriage was the furthest thing from my mind. Besides, I considered my relationship with Thomas great as it was: steady and solid and without strife. We seemed to have found a good rhythm, and for the moment that seemed to be enough.

But as I sat there, giddy with jet lag, overwhelmed with the unexpected proposal, I was incapable of voicing my heartfelt concerns. I did not want to disappoint Thomas.

Thomas lifted the ring from the box and I recognized it; we had seen that ring at the Niessing shop in New York. The ring's design was deceptively simple: a stunning diamond suspended in a band of matte platinum. It was called a tension ring because the diamond was held between the band by nothing but the calibrated tension of the metal. There was no setting. The diamond was suspended in midair, like a jeweler's fabulous magic trick.

Thomas took my hand and slid the ring onto my finger, but when he got to the knuckle, the ring just stopped. "Maybe it's swollen from the flight. Jet lag," I insisted. I pulled my hand away and tried to push the ring farther, but it wouldn't budge. I damned my father who constantly cracked my knuckles when I was a young girl. One of his many practical jokes.

As much as I pushed, the ring wouldn't budge. My finger started to turn red. Thomas looked concerned. "Try it on the other hand," he suggested. "Sometimes one hand is smaller than the other."

But the ring didn't fit. It was obvious; the ring did not fit.

With great force, I pushed the ring past the knuckle on my right hand and proudly declared, "There, it works!" I held my hand in the air and tried to get comfortable with the weight and heft that came with that new piece of jewelry.

Five

MATERIAL WORLD

❧

W e lived down the road from fashion designer Adrienne Vittadini, and directly across the street from a guy who (according to rumor) owned a large industrial food corporation.

The latter (I never actually met the man and only remember seeing him once) had torn down the small ranch-style home that had previously occupied his relatively small parcel of land and built a sprawling pink monstrosity—a veritable McMansion. I took photos of the old ranch before it was razed, capturing it one day after a large snowfall. Surrounded by almost two feet of snow, it looked as though it were being sucked into a sinkhole, and it looked like a doll's house.

That spring more large, monstrous houses started to pepper the landscape, and eventually the area had completed its metamorphosis. We were now officially living in one of the chicest Hamptons neighborhoods.

Houses weren't the only structures peppering the land-scape. Retailers also clamored to occupy space in the increasingly desirable beach community. In 1989, Ralph Lauren, one of the first to recognize the area's burgeoning popularity, opened a freestanding store in East Hampton. By the early 1990s, the Hamptons were flooded with new retailers. An outpost of Saks Fifth Avenue was anchored on a prominent corner in Southhampton town and Linda Dresner opened a smaller version of her eponymous Park Avenue boutique. Banana Republic, Eddie Bauer, Coach, Tiffany's, and others followed.

Before living there, my knowledge of the Hamptons was limited. I had only been there once, in the early eighties, for a photo shoot that took place at the home of another model's boyfriend. The house, as I remember it, was nestled in the woods. The model's boyfriend, who was the owner of the house, appeared to be twice her age. On the drive back to Manhattan, there was a vivid conversation about old money, exclusive estates, and undesirable day-trippers. There was mention of artists who sought the quiet and pristine beaches for inspiration, but absolutely no reference was made to shopping.

A decade later and everything had changed. Like other communities across the country, the Hamptons had started on a trajectory that would come to reflect a national preoccupation with having more, consuming more, and displaying more of the materialistic symbols of success.

Juliet Schor calls this "the new consumerism." In a 1999 essay, she describes it as "upscaling of lifestyle norms; the pervasiveness of conspicuous, status goods and of competition for acquiring them; and the growing disconnect between consumer desires and incomes." How this differs from the ordinary "keeping up with the Joneses" of prior decades is that a comparison of similar means no longer takes place between households — the people next door. Instead, comparisons are made to the lifestyles of the rich and upper middle classes. The gap between who we were and who we wanted to be expanded. Luxury had become the dominant aspiration.

This "hyperconsumption" of luxury goods would become the new standard, the new normal, for the Hamptons.

My lifestyle began to revolve around these new standards of consumption as well.

This first became apparent with purchases for the house.

Suddenly, I found myself weighing the difference between a Maytag and a Miele. Instead of buying ordinary garden furniture, we ordered lounge chairs imported from Spain and a stainless-steel barbecue grill from a prominent German maker. The cappuccino machine was a La Pavoni.

The house's minimalist style dictated the purchase of more modern design furniture than what Thomas had already acquired. He had already built an impressive collection of modern design pieces — expensive and important pieces, I had been told. He had a sofa and chairs from Le Corbusier, a Vico Magistretti bookshelf. Nearly every week we were downtown perusing the SoHo shops and pausing over furniture designed by Eames, Breuer, Grey, and Starck. I hadn't heard of a lot of the stuff and was both bored and mesmerized by it. I realized that I didn't enjoy shopping for furniture as much as I did clothes, but I indulged nonetheless, trying to give myself a quick education. We ended up buying things that had simple designs but interesting-sounding names: Lola Mundo, Fortuny, and Royalton.

When we were contemplating purchasing the Royalton bed, which had been designed by French wunderkind Philippe Starck, the salesperson made sure to point out the singularity of the bed's shiny, pointed metal feet that were molded in the form of what appeared to be large silver horns. I nodded my head in agreement, but to me they looked exactly like those horn-shaped charm necklaces the Italian boys in Staten Island used to wear.

One morning, while standing at the breakfast bar at Sant Ambroeus on Main Street in Southampton, I realized that there was an ex–*Sports Illustrated* swimsuit model to my left and a petite butter-blond Manhattan socialite, who had recently appeared on the pages of *Vogue*, to my right. It was barely ten o'clock, and both were studies in perfection. The former model, cherubic baby in tow, was dressed in the ideal pair of knit track pants worn with a Petit Bateau T-shirt. Her hair, pulled back in a loose ponytail, fell seductively forward as she placed the toddler in his buggy. Her skin was luminous, glowing, and appeared almost supernatural.

As I watched her, I thought, *I think I can do this. I want to try to do this.* I wanted to be as perfect as I believed my new lifestyle demanded me to be. It was the first time I felt I had a foundation in place to achieve this goal. Financially, it was the first time that I was in a position to seek out the best doctors to care for my chronically troubled skin and to afford the best haircuts and color, manicures and pedicures, and gym subscriptions that were necessary. It didn't occur to me at the time that this quest for superficial perfection was a way to protect myself, again, from having to confront my grief and my wobbly sense of identity. To understand any of that, I would have had to reach into the parts of myself I had turned off. I wasn't about to go there. As difficult as physical perfection was, it was easier than looking into the abyss that appeared after my mother's death.

Under these circumstances, I sought the best dermatologist in New York and was put on a three-month course of Accutane. I came away with skin more youthful and perfect than I had ever had. I had doll's skin, a child's skin. The pores had tightened; the flesh had tautened. Now I too had that otherworldly glow.

The next thing I did was change my hairstyle. Out went my long, wavy locks and in came a controlled bob. I stopped getting highlights and let what had formerly been my dark blond hair reveal its new soft chestnut color.

I was experiencing a metamorphosis.

My wardrobe began to morph as well. When Thomas complained about my cutoffs, I had put up a small fight but discarded the old denims. Now, I began to retire all my old clothing on my own. Out went my spandex bicycle shorts, my ruffled blouses, and my skull-and-crossbones charm bracelets. Out went my beloved black leather motorcycle jacket. All these items were boxed up and placed in storage.

Something else about me changed at this time: I found myself falling into the habit of seeking Thomas's approval. Up until that point, I had never sought anyone's approval of my purchases: neither friend nor family nor lovers. The only person I had shopped with on a regular basis had been my mother. But without resisting, I was shopping with Thomas and soliciting the Svengali-like nod, the definitive yes.

I was a pushover at this point, too tired, vulnerable, and insecure to resist. It felt good to fall into the cradle of someone else's care and vision of who I should be.

On visits to Düsseldorf and Hamburg, I loaded up on items from Jil Sander. At the luxurious Jil Sander boutique on Milchstrasse, in the posh outskirts of Hamburg, I stood before the three-way mirror to study myself. I liked the attention lavished on me by the salespeople, the way they buzzed and swooned around me. There, I realized I no longer felt discomfort about that kind of shopping, that kind of attention.

At first, I wasn't sure if the strictness of Jil Sander's designs were my style, but Thomas convinced me that these rigidly tailored outfits suited me. I began to accept, even like, their lack of artifice and strong lines, the no-nonsense menswear fabrics. Besides, Sander was being written up in every fashion magazine. The label was winning accolades from the fashion press. I came to understand that there was a way people reacted to the fact that I wore Jil Sander clothing that was nothing like the way they had reacted to me in the past. People were impressed. In what seemed like a very short period, I had acquired a substantial assortment of Jil Sander clothing. I receded into this clothing and let it shape me rather than allowing myself to shape it.

I also came to enjoy the ritual of shopping at expensive stores. I enjoyed being waited on and being led to a dressing cabin. I enjoyed the way the items I had chosen were handled, like they were delicate specimens. I took pleasure in watching my purchases get folded, boxed, wrapped. Having a handbag placed in a special silk or flannel sack gave me a secret thrill, and seeing a simple white blouse disappear in a cloud of brightly colored tissue paper was as mesmerizing as a magic trick. Even paying was fetishized in a certain style — the receipt itself was printed out on expensive stationery, which was embossed with the label's logo, folded in sharp creases, and placed inside an envelope, the kind of envelope that had a lining, like an expensive skirt.

Thomas also showed me that expensive clothing required expensive care. He taught me how to properly protect my leather handbags and jackets. He bought me an entire set of beautiful black lacquered wooden hangers. There were coat hangers, dress hangers, and hangers that had gold clasps for suit pants. I also got into the habit of making regular trips to the shoe repair to get taps and rubber soles put on each new pair of shoes or boots that I purchased. The shoe repair workers began to recognize me, knew me by name, and sometimes even gave me discounts for being such a regular customer. I finally understood the expression, *well-heeled*.

All this discipline and rigor had a positive effect on me. By allowing myself to shop almost exclusively with Thomas, I was able to manage my uncontrollable shopping self. The phantom shopper I had become after my mother's death—the me who had racked up a few thousand dollars worth of senseless credit card purchases—seemed to have disappeared.

But while it had taken me less than a year to pay off my previous debt, my credit rating would take years to rebuild.

Even though my first foray into acquiring credit cards (with the intention of building a stellar credit rating) turned out disastrously, I was determined to make things right. I maintained my own American Express card, used it infrequently, and paid it off religiously. I stayed away from department store cards completely. For the first time in my life, I felt I approached my financial life responsibly. In addition, when an opportunity came up to take a position as the New York editor for a West Coast fashion trade publication, I was ecstatic. It was the first time in my life I was offered a job where I would have the opportunity to write professionally.

Instead of continuing to do my banking at the credit union where my mother had once worked—that was something from the past, a link to my mother that was still painful—I opened a new bank account for this new financial future.

My sense of well-being during this time was based on

little more than the feeling that acquiring all that "stuff" was somehow indicative of a life going in the right direction. The sole purpose of my paycheck seemed to revolve around having even more purchasing power. The thought of saving any money I earned during that time never occurred to me.

Neither I nor anyone around me questioned where all this buying would lead or what, if anything, it all meant.

So the shopping continued.

I watched the contents of my closet swell and realized that I had more than I could ever have imagined having and probably more than I could wear. Yet I always found myself hankering for more.

I read the new crop of style magazines—*Wallpaper*, *Lucky*, and *Surface*—voraciously, sometimes buying hundreds of dollars worth in a single month, and I always had a list of the things I wanted from their pages.

There were other aspects of my life that changed during this time. Thomas and I began to entertain too, but that didn't always prove easy. I was not as adept at the task as I think he would have liked. This wasn't as simple as stepping into new clothes, and impressing anyone on this front required more skill than shopping.

I had ways of doing things that didn't seem to fit with the new lifestyle. Often there were arguments over what I perceived to be ridiculous things. One time it was the fact that I put smoked salmon and ham on the same serving tray. Another time it was an issue over how I was preparing the chocolate-covered strawberries.

But Thomas was always clear: he liked things a certain

way and was strict about how everything in the house was maintained. He had a proper way of doing everything, from serving a cappuccino to slicing a loaf of bread. I resigned myself to these dictates and tried to adjust to his vision of how things should be. This meant learning how to remove slices of prosciutto from the paper so they didn't break and learning how to serve caviar with a mother-of-pearl spoon. The slate-tiled floor should only be cleaned with sarsaparilla soap. All washing detergents had to be dispensed from their original containers and transferred into slender, brushed aluminum cylinders. The toothpaste tube was always relegated to the cabinet and never, ever left on the edge of the sink. The dishwasher got loaded *this* way.

Each weekend the swimming pool was covered ritualistically with a giant tarpaulin, which would gather heat from the sun while at the same time keeping any detritus from landing in the pristine water. The lawn was mowed each week, and the privet hedge was trimmed on a regular basis as well. When my father came to visit, I had to politely ask him not to lie on the sofa wearing only his swimming trunks. "Skin oils, suntan lotion...they damage the leather." He looked at me as if I were a total stranger.

I hid my messy clutch of notebooks and journals in a closet in one of the spare bedrooms, behind closed doors. And I hid other messy parts of myself as well.

The fact was the house belonged to Thomas, not me. We were engaged, but I just lived there. He had bought it, and he was paying the mortgage. It was his prerogative to be the king of his castle. I never asked exactly where I fit into the picture. Exactly where my security lay was never discussed. "What's mine is yours," Thomas had always said. Legally that didn't hold water. The smart girl I used to be knew that, but at the time the implications were lost on me. I didn't want to think about difficult things, to tussle with realities, to contend with what-ifs. I just wanted to continue on my unconscious pursuit of perfection.

This ability to blot out my former self, my painful emotions, and deny my own autonomy had become impressive. There were only a few times when something managed to intrude. One of those times happened one sunny afternoon when my brother Francis called. I picked up the phone from its cradle and began walking upstairs as we started to speak. I was glad to hear from him, happy to hear his voice. I was anxious to hear what he had to say. But by the time I reached the top of the stairs, the conversation had stopped me dead in my tracks.

"I can't see you anymore," my brother said. "Please don't ask why. Just accept that I am just not going to be able to see you anymore." I can remember standing on the landing and rubbing my bare foot over a patch of sunlight that came through the skylight. The patch of sunlight made a perfect square on the gray carpet. I asked my brother if I had done something wrong.

"No," he insisted forcefully. But he wouldn't elaborate, wouldn't offer any more clarity.

"I don't think you should do this," I pleaded.

"It's just what I need to do right now," he insisted. And then he seemed to want to cut the conversation off. "Well, when will we speak again?" I stupidly asked. He said, "I don't know."

I hung up and immediately felt my head begin to pound; the muscles on the back of my neck constricted. I stood on the landing, frozen, and noticed that the patch of sunlight had moved. Suddenly, the light hurt my eyes, and I began to feel nauseous. I could feel one of my migraines coming on, and so I retreated to the one place I could get closest to total darkness: my closet. I closed the door and lay down on the roughly textured carpet.

I lay still on the floor of my closet. The door was closed, and it was almost completely dark inside but for a sliver of light peeking through the door seams. Surrounding me were all the clothes I had bought in the past decade, or at least half of them. Many of them dangled from a slender silver pole, carefully placed on cherrywood hangers painted in black lacquer. The pants were suspended upside down like a row of ankle-chained Houdinis. On the shelves above my head were several towers of sweaters. There was one tower dedicated to cashmere and one dedicated to vests. There was a tower dedicated to only white T-shirts and another to colored T-shirts. There was a single tower for shorts, running pants, yoga pants, and cargo pants.

Tickling my nostrils was the faint scent of cedar that came from both the shoe trees and the cedar balls that I had placed intermittently along the shelves. I could feel the scratchy carpet embossing its texture on my shoulder blades and the backs of my legs; it was uncomfortable, but I did not move. I let this discomfort have its way with me.

I breathed in the muffled quiet of the clothing that surrounded me. Here, if nothing was stirred, nothing moved. It felt safe.

I stayed there for a long time.

♦ ♦ ♦

I can't remember exactly what summer it was, but it was one of those summers that seemed to melt into the next during those years—the summers of the nineties when the Hamptons seemed to be on an ever-escalating spiral of fabulousness. The houses grew larger; the wealth seemed endless. There seemed to be more celebrities than the summer before, their stardust rubbing off on everything around them. There were charity benefits, polo matches, and parties, and on any given Saturday, Southampton's main street was filled with beautiful people.

Sitting on the bench in front of Sant Ambroeus on a summer afternoon, I felt I'd become a part of this enchantment. It was as if the entire world had opened up and swallowed my former self. I wore a simple white cotton halter dress with a very low back and flat sandals in an off-white buckskin that reminded me of the texture of the saddle shoes I wore when I was on the cheerleading squad in junior high. There was a group of us on the bench outside the restaurant, and we were all eating ice cream, chatting, laughing, bathed in the particles of stardust in the late-afternoon summer light.

This is when I realized that I was shining in that otherworldly way. I had achieved my goal—*I can do this; I think I can do this.* I finally looked the part: perfect, polished, and flawless. I not only belonged there in my appearance, but also in my disposition. I moved, spoke, and laughed a certain way. I had reformatted myself, reconfigured myself. Now I was being accepted in a new way, and this felt strangely exhilarating and constricting at the same time. I felt both pushed and pulled. There was a tautness to me that I did not recognize. But an apparent flexibility too; I realized I had the rubbery ability to adapt myself. Just like my brother had said, I was like a chameleon, changing my colors in order to blend in and stay protected. I had created a new version of myself, and with this realization, I felt like someone had wrapped me in plastic. A suffocating feeling accompanied my revelation.

I had made an outline of myself. The substance of me was put on hold; that would have to be filled in somewhere along the way.

If I did not understand the concept of conspicuous consumption before, I came to understand it fully while indulging in the lifestyle of the Hamptons. The opportunity existed, almost without limitations, to acquire and to display. It was really not more complicated than that. And while it is easy to see this simple equation in retrospect, it was more difficult to distinguish it at the time. To be surrounded by everything that constitutes the good life—the life that was being sold on the pages of magazines, in movies, books and television shows, in shops—is to, at least partially, be out of touch with a larger reality. In my case, this meant being out of touch with the reality of everything that had made me up until that point.

This also became the unfortunate way in which I related to Thomas. I knew him primarily by his possessions—the furniture he had and continued to acquire, the expensive suits he wore, and the car he bought for himself, a rare and beautiful vintage Mercedes-Benz 190SL from 1961.

I don't think I ever really plumbed the depths of Thomas, not in the way one person who shares a full decade of her life with another should. I accepted the surface and let it go at that. Equally, I believed there were entire vistas of me that he never knew existed. This being the case, shopping seemed to take the place of other forms of communication.

Six

FASHIONS OF THE TIMES

⁂

One Saturday morning while watching *Style with Elsa Klensch* on CNN, I caught a glimpse of myself entering the Anna Sui fashion show. In the scrum of editors making their way to assigned seats, there I was, passing ever so briefly, in front of the camera. I wore a red wool vintage-style motoring cap. Beneath this, I had plaited my long, blond hair in Heidi-style braids.

That hat had been bought at Barneys a few days earlier because I wanted something new to wear to 7th on Sixth, the twice yearly fashion shows staged by American designers. It was 1993, and the shows were newly organized under a governing body. Along with their clever new name (Seventh Avenue was home to New York's garment industry, Sixth Avenue was where the shows would be staged), the shows now boasted the support of heavyweight corporate sponsors. Circuslike tents were erected in Bryant Park just off Sixth Avenue. They were filled with row upon row of bleachers to accommodate the hundreds of invitees. More media began to appear; even more photographers and television crews were now on the scene. Celebrities, who had been a rarity at previous fashion shows, now started to stake their claim on front row seating.

Spotting myself on television that morning, however briefly, confirmed my sense that I had found my place. Instinctively, I saw that the self-absorbed and insular fashion world was as detached from reality as I was trying to be. I enjoyed being a part of it, and I enjoyed the false sense of importance it gave me.

I liked everything that went along with being an arbiter of style: assignments to interview industry players, invitations to parties, attending the shows. Vera Wang offered to create a black wedding dress for me, and I could almost feel my ego inflate—*a customized wedding dress from Vera Wang... and black no less.* I found myself in meetings with Bill Blass or at a luncheon in honor of the Italian designer Valentino.

By the next season, as I walked down Sixth Avenue toward Bryant Park to attend the shows, I could feel the electricity in the air. It was like a drug. From several blocks away, I could see the tips of the white tents come into view. As I got closer, I could hear the tom-tom beat of the DJ's tunes. Then there was the shuffle and bustle at the venue's entrance, the importance of being allowed entry. I liked that sense of importance. It was the same as I had felt as a teenager when I was let into Studio 54. It was the same superficial sizing up, only transposed to a new decade, a new venue, and a different industry.

And since this was the case, each season as fashion week approached, I added new items to my wardrobe. Much of that shopping was predicated on the fact that I sought the approval of this microcosmic world that I was now part of. I understood that as a fashion writer, attending 7th on Sixth was one part seeing the collections and one part being seen.

With that in mind, I bought new items for my wardrobe. I purchased the red hat and a pair of black oversized Cutler and Gross sunglasses (which Thomas deemed "ridiculous") because all the editors were wearing those big black glasses that season. In another moment of extreme retail neediness, I sat in Barneys and forced my feet into a pair of knee-high black leather motorcycle boots. The next day I suffered through five solid hours of shows with my toes in a knot. The boots fit poorly, and I could hardly walk. I returned to Barneys and traded them in for a shorter version of the same style because that's how desperate I was to be wearing the cool boots.

In the seasons that followed, each time fashion week rolled around, my outfits became more meticulously constructed. As I had forfeited any personal style for Thomas's approval, I also gave up my personal style in order to be accepted by the fashion tribe. My purchases became linked to the trend of the day, the look that was being shown on the runway, and the labels that were getting the most press. The individuality of my former wardrobe—my mix-and-match style, flea market finds, Army surplus relics, and quirky combinations—was gone. I was molding myself into another perfect image: the fashion writer of the nineties.

♦

Working in the fashion industry expanded my shopping spectrum. Not only did I shop to dress for the twice yearly runway shows, but I now had to shop for things to wear to the myriad black tie events I found myself attending.

I never imagined I would have a selection of evening gowns hanging in my closet. Yet one day, there they were. I owned gowns that had weight and heft. I had gowns that demanded space and needed to be suspended from their own special satin-padded hangers. There were hangers entwined in beautiful pale pink satin, looking as delicate as a ballerina's toe shoes; hangers that came with their own pearl-tipped push pins with which the thinnest of spaghetti straps could be secured. Sometimes it made me wistful just to look at those hangers. Even more than the gowns themselves, the hangers seemed to possess a divine purpose and a fragile beauty that always caught me by surprise.

Many of the gowns I bought during this time were black. There was a black satin-backed crepe dress, with a low-cut back and a space-agey silver ring neck piece. It was purchased at the Charivari boutique on 57th Street. There was a sober black wool column, from Jil Sander, that fell past my ankles into a puddle on the floor, in the style of Morticia Addams from the Addams family. That dress was bought in Rome. Then, on a trip to Barneys, I bought a Comme des Garçons black silk gown with frayed ("distressed") edges around the collar and cuffs of the sleeves. The model Linda Evangilista had worn that very dress on the cover of *Harper's Bazaar* magazine.

I wore the Comme des Garçons gown to an event at the Metropolitan Museum of Art, in the Temple of Dendur. It was an event celebrating shoes. How ridiculous that sounds in retrospect, but at the time, it felt like such an important part of my work. What I remember about that night was that I stood in a magnificent room feeling more than a little awe-struck by the ancient Egyptian temple, the reflecting pool, and the expansive wall of glass that looked out on to Central Park. There was an army of waiters waltzing into the room, shouldering silver trays. Upon each tray was a dessert made of gold spun sugar and dark chocolate molded into the shape of a stiletto. I received numerous compliments on my dress that evening, and almost everyone recognized it from the cover of the magazine.

The following year, same event, my outfit was not as successful. I decided to wear the shirt my brother Francis had given me for my fourteenth birthday. As much as I sought to bury my old self, I had lapses of sentimentality that manifested in my wardrobe choices. I had kept that shirt over the years as a symbol of my love for my brother and had an urge to wear it, especially since he was absent from my life. The shirt was a sleeveless knit the color of putty that was embellished with a bib of artificial gemstones. That evening, I paired it with a floor-length black crepe skirt. Despite how content I was to be wearing my vintage gift, several friends said I looked tired. The ensemble did not win any compliments.

As much as I tried to keep this urge at bay, my wistfulness about various pieces of clothing seemed to be a repeating pattern. I can recall attending a press dinner at a palazzo in Florence, Italy, where, as I stood at the foot of a very large marble staircase, it occurred to me that a palazzo was, in fact, a palace. Of course, I knew this. But in that moment, it registered as a piece of new and vital information, and it was accompanied by a vision of my mother dancing around the cramped Brooklyn apartment of my childhood in her black satin palazzo pants. At first, this vision felt like a current running through me, but afterward I was filled with such a longing for my mother's presence that I could barely get through the rest of the evening.

Later, in my hotel room, I told myself that identifying an individual with their clothing in this way was faulty. Of course, no one, not one of us, is defined by what we wear. Yet we are what we wear, at least to a certain degree. In the years since my mother's death, I had kept her black satin palazzo pants tucked away in my closet. I had never worn them and hardly ever looked at them. Still, when I came across them in the back of the closet, I was always reminded of the joy with which she wore them.

That evening, I realized that my mother had never been to Italy. She had never been in a palazzo. She would never see my closet full of evening gowns.

♦ ♦ ♦

There were other privileges that came with being a member of the fashion press, such as receiving samples from new collections that were not yet available in stores. At luncheons and press launches, goody bags were left on every seat, handed out to every guest. Being a member of the press meant that I was often privy to some of the most coveted New York sample sales, sometimes days before they were opened to the public.

Sample sales always invited a certain mania. Just the idea that ordinarily astronomically priced designer fashions could be picked up at bargain prices could spark an adrenaline rush. But while I loved the sample sale as concept, I often found myself overwhelmed by the actual experience. The best sample sales were inevitably overcrowded, push-and-shove affairs that required both stamina and preparation. Dressing for this particular shopping required a strategy: easy-on, easy-off outfits; a base of tights and no transparent brassieres; no jewelry that might get caught on delicate fabrics, closures, and zippers; and slip-on shoes. This, of course, didn't stop me from attending.

After a few years my closet was brimming with sample sale finds, the most coveted of which were items from the labels Lagerfeld, Trussardi, Burberry, Alberta Ferretti, Jean Paul Gaultier, and Dior. However, even though I ended up acquiring some of the most beautiful items I'd ever owned at these sales, they were not the most treasured of my shopping experiences.

What I began to treasure most was a shopping style similar to that which I had adopted immediately after my mother's death. It was that trancelike shopping, where I could put myself in an almost hypnotic state. In this state, I was able to fill entire afternoons by simply drifting through shops. I found I could cocoon myself in those moments and would end up achieving an almost submerged quiet, as if I were floating in my own personal fish tank.

One day, I spent hours in the lingerie department of Bloomingdale's. Another time, I took cover from the rain on the second and third floors of Saks. It was pouring out, miserably cold, and the safest place I could think to be was in the hushed corridors, amid the racks of clothing, in the calm that prevailed on the sales floor in the middle of a weekday afternoon. I stayed there for hours that day and eventually left with a black-and-white-checked waistcoat, yet another item from the French designer Jean Paul Gaultier. It had a satin back and a row of gray mother-of-pearl buttons. I remember it costing around four or five hundred dollars.

I began to lie to Thomas about how I spent my afternoons. I lied casually, without much thought of what it meant or if there might be consequences. Sometimes, I would mention things I had purchased but leave out any details: price and how much time I had actually spent in the store. Other times, I would not mention the shopping at all. If asked, I would say I was at a lunch, had a meeting, or went to a museum. I felt protective of this shopping, as if it were something that needed to be isolated from any outside influence — as if it were something that could only belong to me. I didn't want to share.

I became comfortable with these lies. I was shocked by how easily I could manufacture them and how readily they were accepted. I started to indulge in more secret shopping.

♦

One time, when I had a few hours to kill between two 7th on Sixth fashion shows, I went into Saks with no particular intention. As I made my way across the busy ground floor, through the hectic cosmetics department, I suddenly felt as if I had been enveloped in an invisible force field. I felt a heightened awareness, as if my senses had been turned up. Everything appeared illuminated, bathed in a sunny glow. I felt more alive, buoyant, and as if my physical proportions were magnified.

These sensations made me panic. What I felt was that I had to buy something. It was similar to an impulse I began to have when I drove a car—an impulse to stop the car by driving it into the guardrail or a tree or any stationary object that would make the vehicle come to a halt.

Whenever I drove, I had to concentrate on controlling the impulse and talk myself away from it. It was like trying to talk a jumper off a window ledge. Ultimately, I never crashed the car, but that strange impulse was undeniable and frightening.

In Saks that day, I felt the same peculiar invasion—a notion that lodged itself inside me and refused to leave—*buy something; you must.*

When I reached the escalator, I realized my palms were sweating, and I rubbed them dry on my jeans. I tried to convince myself it was the fashion shows—a residual high from the tents, from the pomp and circumstance, the photo flash and fluster of the runway presentations.

I ended up purchasing a pair of Dries Van Noten, rayon and wool menswear-inspired trousers that hung low on my hips and had a long, wide leg. I also bought a Dolce & Gabbana wool polo sweater with short sleeves in the same eggplant color. Together, the two items were close to $1,000.

The gap between wanting and having was no longer present; it had ceased to exist somewhere along the way. Although I could not afford to have everything my heart desired, I found myself with a lifestyle in which I was able to purchase most of what I wanted. I wore clothing that was on the pages of fashion magazines and could shop anywhere I wished, and something about this started to make me feel uncomfortable.

However, the gap that bothered me was the gap between what I was pretending to want and what I truly wanted. The more Thomas and I discussed marriage and starting a family, the more anxious I became. Something was wrong with the picture I was painting myself into, and as much as I wanted it all to make sense, it didn't. I kept waiting for something to click into place.

I woke one day convinced that I needed a break from my relationship. I had decided to make the change because I felt cornered and trapped and confused. I told Thomas what I wanted to do. There wasn't anything to explain. I just needed some time to figure out how to make the next step. I felt greedy and ungrateful, because the truth was that Thomas had done nothing wrong. He provided everything he thought he was supposed to provide. "What is it you're always search-ing for?" he asked.

"I'm searching for myself," I answered. I had rehearsed that line repeatedly, but when finally spoken, it sounded melodramatic, almost comical.

"You are like a blind person, bumping around in the dark," Thomas said.

Before I even had a chance to change my mind, he informed me that he'd found himself a short-term furnished apartment across town.

As Thomas moved into his new temporary apartment, I went on a business trip to Paris.

Almost immediately after my flight landed, I found myself standing in L'Eclarieur, a boutique in the Marais dis-trict of Paris, trying on a black wool double-breasted pants suit from Prada.

"Here, put these on," the skinny boy trying to sell me the suit instructed. He placed a pair of black Prada pumps with a square toe and high, chunky heel on the floor. I slipped my bare feet into the shoes.

"It looks fantastic," he squealed.

There I was again: another suit, another city, another several thousand dollar price tag. Only this time things were a little different. Thomas and I were officially split, and I no longer enjoyed the benefits of his generosity. Although I had started paying rent on our Midtown apartment while we were a couple, now that we lived apart, I had to pick up the cost of all my living expenses. Realistically, a Prada suit was not in my budget.

But *budget* was not a word I wanted to hear. I did not want to understand the limitations of "live within your means." I had become too accustomed to a certain style of shopping and wanted to continue on that track.

Wearing the suit and the shoes, I surveyed myself in the full-length mirror and had the same physical sensations that had started to appear back in New York. I felt nervous and excited and could feel my palms sweating. I could hear the conversation of a couple standing behind me amplified. The store's lights seemed brilliant, theatrical.

"Could you possibly get me a glass of water?" I asked the skinny boy.

I paced back and forth in front of the mirror. The jacket had a swell belt, with a silver military-style buckle, that sat just on the hips. The name *Prada* had been etched on the belt's metal surface. The pants had a straight tapered leg. The shoes were the final perfect detail, their squared toe adding the precise blunt balance to the look.

He returned with a glass of water, and I took a long, slow sip.

"I have to have this," I said, as I handed the glass back to the boy.

"I think you do," he answered.

The next evening, I wore the suit to a house party. I had been invited as the guest of an executive at Louis Vuitton, someone I had been introduced to through my friend Kendall. The party was in a crowded apartment, in a part of Paris I didn't know. My most vivid memory of that evening is sitting in a small cluster of guests around a coffee table that was piled high with art and photography books. The suit made me feel attractive and clever, and I probably said many things that weren't nearly as witty as I thought they were.

After the party, I returned to my hotel room and hung the suit in the tiny closet. It sat just beneath the incandescent bulb and looked almost iconic, like something that held some special powers, the costume of a superhero.

The French word for suit is *costume*. My mother had always worn those fabulous costumes when she and my father were heading out to a Halloween party. They liked to dress up, to pretend they were something other than what they were. I had worn something that resembled a costume the last time I saw my friend Dr. Miyamoto. He had looked at me disapprovingly.

That night in my hotel, I went to sleep happy that I had my Prada suit—my Prada *costume*—even though I was certain that the purchase would throw my finances into a tailspin.

It was true; I was searching. But every time I searched for myself, I came up with nothing. I searched for myself in suits, in cities, in relationships, but my searching yielded nothing more than a vague, nagging sense that something critical about me was missing. Every time I tried to imagine a life on my own, I couldn't. There didn't seem to be enough of me there. When I looked in my closet, I asked myself: *How can a woman with a closet so full feel so empty inside?*

This emptiness propelled me back into the relationship with Thomas. I became convinced that the only solution was to marry and start a family. Already in my thirties, time was running out.

I returned to New York, resigned and repentant and ready for change. I would quit my job at the newspaper and start freelance work. Thomas suggested I spend more time at the beach house. "It's a good place for you to write," he said. I did not disagree. These all sounded like fabulous opportunities. I would have had difficulty trying to deny that this was the life almost everyone in Manhattan claimed to be dreaming of.

At the same time, we moved to a larger apartment in the same luxury high-rise building. This one now had two bedrooms and two bathrooms. It was wonderfully spacious, and there was enough room for me to set up my office and write a novel. I had a wall of custom-made bookshelves made for my office, and we bought some new furniture to complete the room: an arts-and-crafts table and an antique file cabinet. This was now a "room of my own," a space in which I could create. However, before I could embark on any of the creative writing I so longed to do, I had to contend with my inability to become pregnant.

Infertility had never entered my mind. I had always believed, like many New York women, that I was the one calling the shots. I was in control of when and how I would become pregnant, as I had imagined myself in control of my appearance, my career, and my relationship. I had been able to set these things into something that resembled order and expected to be able to exert the same influence on pregnancy, whenever I set my mind to it.

I hadn't thought much about the miscarriage I had the year of my mother's death, but suddenly I found myself forced to retell the story. Were you ever pregnant? Yes. What happened? Well, I was very thin, very stressed, in a difficult marriage.... I had not spoken about those events and was content to leave them sleeping in the past.

When I found myself sitting in the office of one of New York's most esteemed fertility specialists, listening carefully as he tried to explain "unexplained infertility," I also began to notice that something about me had changed: I had come back into the relationship with Thomas accompanied by a dullness, a lack of feeling. It was similar to the numbness I felt after my mother's death.

As I listened to the doctor speak, I could hardly muster any emotion about my situation or the battery of tests he was prescribing.

◆ ◆ ◆

My friend Kendall tucked a note into the Louis Vuitton book commemorating *"Un Siècle et des Lumières."* It read: "You go to all the right parties and know all the right people." The parties, having taken place in key cities around the world, celebrated "A Century of Monogram: 1896–1996." The book was a gift to all the "right people" who were fortunate enough to have attended. I happened to be one of them. By 1997, the next year, label fever was reaching its zenith, and there I was bouncing around in the mosh pit of luxury-goods lovers.

Toward the end of the decade, there was a giddiness that seemed to have taken hold of Manhattan. It mixed with the oxygen in the air. There was opportunity, optimism, and froth: an endless stream of all the right parties and all the right people.

I flew to Paris for a weekend, expressly to attend another Vuitton bash, where I wore a Rifat Ozbek gown with a bodice ornamented with tiny mirrors. There I was, at cocktails, mingling with Gérard Depardieu, Rupert Everett, Béatrice Dalle, and Vivienne Westwood. Later, I sat through dinner watching, dumbstruck, the extravagant presentation that featured the bizarre Vuitton presentation, a commingling of live animals, contortionists, and one-of-a-kind handbags. The event was luxe and lavish and completely surreal.

Later that evening, I ended up at a house party in Saint-Germain, where I literally sat at Westwood's feet, listening to her pontificate on everything from fashion history to philosophy. I sat there like a lowly fashion disciple, hanging on her every word. Listening to Westwood's musings was entertaining, although some of what she said sounded nonsensical. This only added to the *Through the Looking-Glass* quality of the entire evening. Still, I shouldn't have been perched on the floor at her feet. I should have lifted myself up from that floor. It was undignified.

Eventually, I did leave, but not before the party's host

tried making a drunken pass at me by the front door. I ended up standing in the misty rain, trying to hail a cab, not realizing that I was only around the corner from my hotel.

There were other parties in Milan and Forte dei Marmi and of course New York. There was always a party in New York. Each day when I opened my mailbox, a cascade of invitations came tumbling forward. There was an endless flood of launches: a new fragrance, the introduction of a new collection, the opening of a new store, a private sale, a sneak peak, a new restaurant with a tasting from an acclaimed superstar chef. It seemed to take little or no effort to get a crowd together. And there was almost always a crowd, pushing and shoving in a crush at the door, waving invites in the air as some kind of banner of importance, getting approved by the PR flunkies with their headsets and clipboards, doing their face patrol. The red velvet ropes doing their intimidation things. And the photographers... there always had to be photographers on hand to record the whole thing, because that kind of evidence could help make everything seem more real.

◆ ◆ ◆

In one of her witty and acerbic essays about the myriad characters that toiled in the late twentieth-century fashion industry, the writer Julie Burchill says that people who follow fashion past the age of thirty are truly sad. "I have met some boring people in my life," she writes. "But none as boring as the fashion writer in her thirties."

That's what I had been, a fashion writer in my thirties.

However, sadness is not what I felt in those early days when I stood outside the steps of the New York Public Library clutching my invite in my hands. I can remember feeling elated because Anna Wintour noticed my cool suit or Bill Cunningham wanted to take my picture for the *New York Times* or because I had the chance to sit at Vivienne Westwood's feet. The swirl and excitement of the shows and the shopping that went with them were pacifiers, distractions that were easy to latch on to.

As the decade was ending, I had begun to understand sadness and boredom. The fashion industry was becoming a cliché of the worst, most negative stereotypes. I was starting to wake up from my self-exile, from my mad dash for cover under the blanket of perfection that I had stayed in for far too long. I knew I still loved fashion, but I no longer was in love with the fashion industry.

As 1998 ended, the 7th on Sixth spring 1999 collections were being shown. General Motors Fashion Week, as it was now called, once again took place in Bryant Park. The organized shows were five years old and an undeniable success. Not only were there more shows on the roster than ever before, but attendance and media coverage were peaking as well. A television show, *7th on Sixth: Inside Fashion Week,* hosted by the model Lauren Hutton, was due to air in December.

But I no longer felt compelled to shop for the shows as I once had. I could hardly muster the effort to attend more than a handful. I would show up at the pressroom to get my identification badge and my overstuffed tote bag filled with promotional products, and then retreat to my apartment with bounty in tow. I would spread the gifts on my bed and pick through them, analyzing what each product meant: Crest Whitestrips, Dr. Scholl's gel insoles, a makeup mirror, a *New York Times Magazine* T-shirt, a box of chocolates, a new wrinkle cream.

The next season while attending the shows, I found the scene had morphed into something unrecognizable. It had become so distorted, overwrought, and overblown; its purpose seemed entirely unclear. Was the show season about presenting clothing to the fashion press and retailers anymore? Or had it just become a circus of singular personalities, performing for the ever-present camera?

Fashion had become too fashionable.

The scene was now an orgy of commotion, a chaotic cabaret. A moat of video trucks, news vans, and chauffeur-driven limousines surrounded Bryant Park. An army of sentrylike security guards stood, arms crossed, at every venue entrance. It's not surprising that the word *fashionista* came into use. The whole event had a militaristic feel. The tom-tom beat of a DJ's selection could be heard reverberating above the drone of city traffic, louder than ever, louder than I remembered. The crowds were bigger than ever too and had to be corralled, contained: *those with seats to the left; standing room to the right.*

Two books that were published later that year captured the zeitgeist: Bret Easton Ellis's *Glamorama* and Jay McInerney's *Model Behavior*. Both made the case that fashion had replaced drugs as the defining cultural pulse point of the decade.

Yes, it was true. Fashion was the drug at the end of the millennium and shopping its handmaiden.

Rather than be excited by this, I wanted to skulk away, to ply my trade writing exclusively about fashion photography rather than fashion or to console myself within the folds of novel writing. Or maybe I knew that I just could no longer keep up with the increasing demands. The fashion industry was never known for its loyalty; it was a system that required constant renewal, constant irrigation.

Or perhaps it was my own renewal that was necessary. Was I the one who had changed? Had something come loose in my own moorings? Had something inside me finally broken at last? I was not certain. I only knew that I could console myself with the fashion world as a place to hide.

Seven

THE PRICE OF EVERYTHING, THE VALUE OF NOTHING

---~✕~---

In retrospect, I can see the inevitability of my perfect life falling to pieces. It was impossible to maintain. The elaborate theater play had started to unravel. Since my return from Paris with my Prada suit and my new resignation, I had been growing increasingly unhappy.

I was trying to start a family but realized those attempts were misguided. I was planning a wedding, but my heart could not have been further from that task. Perhaps out of frustration, because we couldn't manage to construct wedding plans, Thomas and I began wearing wedding bands. So in addition to having my diamond tension ring on my right hand, I now had a slender platinum wedding band on my left hand. This too was superficial.

Yes, my shored-up self was starting to come undone, but I continued to turn to shopping to appease my discomfort.

One day, while trawling the aisles of Saks I found an

unlined gray wool coat. It had grommets under the armpits and a flap closure at the neck that made it look somewhat militaristic, or maybe even Army surplus, but in the most elegant of possible ways. It fell just below the knee and had two huge patch pockets, and there was something vaguely vagabond about it, although the price tag was anything but.

The coat was on sale, but it still rung in at several hundred dollars. I tried it on, and before the fabric had settled on my shoulders, I knew I had to have it. The tone of gray complemented the gray pinstripe Armani pants I wore, but also, something about it just felt right. Instead of having the coat placed in a bag, I asked the sales associate to remove the price tag and I wore it out of the store; the leather jacket I had been wearing was placed in the Saks Fifth Avenue bag instead.

I was on my way to the New York University hospital to have another test; just another in a battery of tests to figure out why I could not get pregnant. This one was to be a hysterosalpingogram, and I was told it would not be painful. But I already knew this was not the truth, having experienced pain from the most routine of gynecological exams.

I rode the elevator up to the third floor, registered myself, and waited in the soothing moss-colored waiting room for my name to be called. I kept my new coat on the entire time. The wool's crispness reminded me of an Army blanket my father used to have. After about fifteen minutes, I was called into the examination room.

The room was large, dimly lit, but solidly sterile and cold. Everything about it was cold. The machinery was impressive in its sheer volume; there seemed to be metal contraptions everywhere, all stealth and silence and icy surfaces. There was a cold-looking metal table smack in the center of the room.

The technician, a slender black girl with braided hair piled high on her head, asked me to disrobe, change into the paper dress—*opening to the front, please*—and wait on the cool metal centerpiece.

As I lay there waiting for the technician to return, I thought of a paper dress I had once bought at Patricia Field down on 8th Street. I was going to a wedding with my friend David and wanted to buy something new to wear, but didn't have much money. I went to Patricia Field because I thought I'd find a quirky item—a dress or skirt—to pair with something I already owned.

This was in the early eighties, when shopping at her downtown boutique was great fun, if not for the clothing, but also for the eclectic salespeople she employed. She liked to hire graffiti artists, skater kids, and transvestites, who all added to the subversive feeling of the place.

The day I went there with David, I found the paper dress, and I can still remember spotting it, dangling from a hanger, with its peculiar stiffness and lightness captivating me. The dress was a very light blue, just like the paper dresses in doctors' offices and hospitals. The bottom part of the dress, the skirt, was cut in a full circular shape, and the top was a simple sleeveless bodice with a crew neckline.

"You're not going to buy that," my friend David chided, and he touched the paper disapprovingly. He rubbed the hem between his thumb and forefinger and laughed as he did this.

"Why not?" I insisted. "I think it's great. It's paper. Can you imagine, a paper party dress!"

The dress was in my budget, so I bought it and ended up wearing it to the wedding with a cardigan sweater and ankle-strap sandals. I felt special because everyone was talking about the dress, but by the end of the evening, some guy had managed to burn a hole near the hem with his lit cigarette. The dress had to be trashed.

After a few minutes, the technician came back into the room and asked me to scoot down to the edge of the table and place my legs in the stirrups. She ran through details of the procedure and then reminded me, rather unemotionally, that it would not hurt.

It did hurt, and when I began to cry out in pain, she told me to breathe deeply and that it would be over in a matter of seconds. When the longest "matter of seconds" had passed, I realized there were tears running down my cheeks and my fists were clenched. "That's it; you did great," she said, as she turned off the overhead lamp.

"Oh, and the results of the test are positive," she said, meaning it appeared there was no blockage. This was good news, but it still left my inability to conceive a big question mark.

Dressed, bill paid, and finished with the latest ordeal, I got into the elevator.

A handsome doctor got into the elevator with me, and we rode down in silence until, as the doors were about to open, he turned to me and said, "Nice coat."

What did that remark, those two little words, stir in me?

As I left the hospital, I realized that my attitude about shopping had changed over the years. When I had bought the blue paper party dress, it was with joy and abandon. There was a budget, and my search for something to wear within that budget left me happy when I discovered that I could afford the paper dress. There was laughter and amusement in my memory of purchasing that dress. I remember deriving real pleasure from wearing it too.

By the end of the 1990s, when I was in a situation where I could buy almost anything I wanted, my shopping had become distorted and at times inexplicable. There was my Cosabella incident: the purchase of twenty pairs of underwear and the regret-filled aftermath. And then the incident at Saks: sweaty palms and vertigo.

No longer consuming, just being consumed.

And there was something I came to call "hoarding," which I had started to do on a regular basis. Hoarding was a habit of purchasing something and then not allowing myself to wear it until an identical replacement had been purchased. It wasn't as simple as buying multiples of a garment. At times, I would do that too. The hoarding ritual was unique and disturbing, because hoarding meant buying something, displaying it prominently in my closet, and denying myself the pleasure of wearing it until the replacement had been purchased.

Along with this, and also equally disturbing, were all the items bought but never used. Like Warhol, I had a cache of unopened bags at the bottom of my closet. Like half of Manhattan, I shopped every day.

What was understood, even if unspoken, was that shopping took up an enormous space in the lives of Manhattanites. And it wasn't just ordinary shopping; it was extreme shopping, binge shopping, retail therapy.

By the middle of the decade, Manhattan was blanketed with luxury retailers. The "it" bag—the desirable status handbag that everyone wanted—appeared, as well as the it girls who carried them. Handbags had names like children. They were desired and coveted, and there were long waiting lists to get one.

Toward the end of the decade, I was waking up from my unconscious self. I had started to have my strange shopping episodes, had started to spend secret time shopping, and had started to feel hermetically sealed in my perfect life.

During this time, there were two things I noticed that left an indelible impression on me: One was a cartoon in the *New Yorker* magazine that showed a well-dressed woman panhandling on a street corner with the sign NEED FENDI SHOES TO GO WITH FENDI BAG. I never cut cartoons out of the *New Yorker*, but that one I did. I kept it tacked on a wall of my office. And in 1997, Cool Shoppin' Barbie, a joint venture between Mattel and MasterCard, was introduced. Each Barbie came with her own MasterCard and unlimited play "credit" as well as a register that prompted Barbie to say "thank you" and "credit approved" after each swipe of her card.

♦ ♦ ♦

What was a shopping addict anyway? How would I know if I was one? There is a simple test for determining if you have a compulsive shopping disorder. It's an easy "if you answer yes to any of these questions" kind of test. The questions are roughly along the following lines: Do you get a rush from shopping? Do you buy things you don't need? Do you hide your purchases? Do you use money that should be spent on bills to make other unnecessary purchases? Do you feel guilt, shame, or regret about your spending?

Simply put, shopping addiction is shopping that impacts life in a negative way, according to myriad Web sites and magazine articles that now exist on the subject. Some texts say that shopping addiction is related to poor self-esteem, to a desire to lift moods or a desire to get control.

Dr. April Benson, a New York–based psychiatrist specializing in the treatment of shopping disorders, offers a succinct definition in the introduction to her book *I Shop, Therefore I Am: Compulsive Buying and the Search for Self,* where she writes: "This disorder is often linked to emotional deprivations in childhood....There is a clear correlation between addictive consumption tendencies and the extent to which people perceive that the shopping experience and the goods purchased can make them feel good and appear socially desirable. Said simply, compulsive buying seems to represent search for self in people whose identity is neither firmly felt nor dependable."

Benson reveals that although the stereotypical compulsive shopper image is of "a thirtysomething female who experiences irresistible urges, uncontrollable needs, or mounting tension that can be relieved only by the compulsive buying of clothing, jewelry, and cosmetics," this view, in fact, only covers a small portion of the compulsive buyer spectrum. Benson, through her New York practice and extensive research, finds that the spectrum of compulsive buyers runs across age, gender, and socioeconomic lines.

As to determining the prevalence of the addiction in the United States, a 2006 Stanford University research study shows an average of 6 percent of the U.S. population fits the "compulsive-buyer build." Other estimates see compulsive shopping disorder affecting anywhere from as low as 2 percent to more than 12 percent of the population.

Dr. Donald Black, professor of psychiatry at the University of Iowa College of Medicine, focuses his research on the subject of age and concludes that the age of onset for compulsive buying disorder appears to be in the late teens to early twenties, with a mean age of onset being thirty. He goes on to speculate that the onset corresponds with emancipation from the family home and the period during which people first establish credit accounts.

Other characteristics of compulsive shoppers include

the following: They often like to shop alone and may make extensive preparations for shopping trips. They describe shopping experiences as exciting and sometimes even leading to sexual feelings. Yet when a purchase is completed, feelings change to disappointment, anger, and self-criticism. Typical items purchased include clothing, shoes, compact discs, jewelry, cosmetics, and household items.

Black and others also support the theory that there are varying degrees of severity of compulsive shopping disorder as well as a variety of compulsive shopping styles ranging from daily shopping to binge shopping, image spending, bulimic spending (buying and returning), codependent spenders, compulsive gifting, collecting, and bargain hunting.

Which one was I?

◆ ◆ ◆

In 2000, when my grandmother died, my brother Francis surprised everyone by showing up at the wake. After an absence of nearly a decade, there he was, standing at the back of the very room where my mother had been laid out years earlier. When I saw him, I behaved like someone in a movie, running toward him, hugging him hard, and shaking my head in disbelief.

He grabbed me by the arm and pulled me out of the room. There, in the empty corridor of the funeral home, he began to show me his tattoos. He didn't say a word about where he had been or what had happened in his life. He lifted the sleeve of his shirt to expose a large, sprawling colorful tattoo.

"Here, look at this," he said, and he began to show me all the illustrations he had inked onto his flesh.

If it weren't so bizarre, it would have been comical. But what I remember most is that it practically made me queasy; it almost made me sick. I tried to get him to stop, asked questions to which there was no reply. "Here, look at this one," he said. I have no memory of what those tattoos looked like because in that moment I was overcome with the blinding realization that my brother and I were exactly alike. Over the decade, he too had retreated into a cocoon, a place to hide from his grief. He too had made an outline of himself.

Old wounds were reopened and fresh wounds appeared once I was reunited with my brother. His presence only cast a further critical light on the choices I'd made in my own life. The unease I felt in my home, in my perfect life, now felt compounded by his presence.

The next time I saw him was at a birthday party for my nephew Ben, my brother Stephan's son. It was held at our childhood home, which now belonged to Stephan. My father had remarried, moved to New Jersey with his new wife, and sold Stephan the house lock, stock, and barrel. This arrangement made me uncomfortable, but I had been afraid to voice an objection.

Now Francis was back, and for the first time in many years, we found ourselves together in the house in which we'd grown up. We were in the basement, which hadn't changed much from the way I remembered it. It was cluttered with mementos from our childhoods: schoolbooks and notepads, a broken clock radio, a doll with a knob of hair that grew out of the top of her head. On a heap of old magazines stood a pair of my old wedgies with a teakwood platform that looked almost five inches high. These made us laugh. "How did I ever walk in those things?" I held the shoes in my hands. The rust suede vamps had hardened over the years and were as rough as sandpaper.

I watched Francis as he looked through a stack of old LPs that used to belong to our parents, and when he came across an original recording of *West Side Story,* I saw his eyes light up.

"Take it," I told him. "You should have it."

He looked at me doubtfully and said, "I have to ask Stephan."

"Well, ask, but it shouldn't be a problem," I insisted.

Believing that Francis and I were suffering our mother's absence in similar ways, I felt he should have things that reminded him of her. I felt angry, as I watched him put it back in the pile.

"Take it," I insisted. "Really." I grabbed it and placed it in his hands.

As we mounted the stairs, Stephan suddenly appeared at the landing.

"I wanted to have this," Francis said sheepishly, and he thrust the worn record album forward for approval.

Then to the surprise of us both, without even looking at it, Stephan objected. He continued to speak, something about "I bought the house. Well, let me think about it," but I found it impossible to listen. I watched Francis's face and caught the fleeting stab of pain that crossed it.

In that moment, I saw our family's tragedy come into

sharp focus: the brutality of my mother's sudden death and relentless absence and the silence that had fallen over us all. With a lack of any real dialogue, Stephan had been appointed curator of our former lives; he had been given free rein over all the family's possessions.

Francis didn't argue. He simply placed the LP on a side table in the hallway and headed toward the backyard to the party.

I was the one brimming with anger. Following Francis into the backyard, I stood in front of my father and lashed out into an incomprehensible rant of my own. Then I ran into the house, into the dining room, and looking around the room, wild-eyed, I grabbed a painting that Francis had bought for my mother just before she died. She had never seen the painting. It had ended up in the house because Francis had brought it there when there was still hope that she might one day return from the hospital. She never did. The painting had sat in that same corner for years. It sat in that corner even when the room had been painted and redecorated. The glass on the frame was splattered with small dots of paint. Each time I had come to visit, the painting was there, and it was a painful reminder of both my mother and Francis's absence. It was both neglected and constantly noticed.

With the painting tucked under my arm, I stormed out of the house, Thomas by my side. We got in the car and tore down the street like Bonnie and Clyde.

Why was I making such a big deal out of an old LP and a painting? Why was I risking a rift with my father and my eldest brother when there was nothing really of importance to raise a stink over? And why was I so concerned about my brother having something from that house with all its dust-covered memories?

Francis was the one who seemed to be able to put ice in his veins when it became necessary. I was the one who made a scene like a crazy lady, took off with Thomas like Bonnie and Clyde, while Francis stayed at the party, sat back in the lounge chair, and calmly popped open another beer.

When I returned to my apartment, I ordered a CD of the *West Side Story* sound track for my brother Francis and had it sent to his apartment, even though I knew this was meaningless. The importance of the LP was the connection to our mother, to our childhoods, and to our memories of her and what they meant. A new CD was meaningless; it was simply music.

In the meantime, the painting was cleaned up. Thomas had painstakingly removed all the tiny paint splatters and had delivered the spic-and-span version to its new home on the wall of my office. I hadn't intended to keep the painting; I wanted to give it back to Francis, who I believed was its rightful owner. But he insisted that he didn't want it. So it ended up being mine.

At first, I thought the painting was a symbol of my mother, but since my mother had never seen it, had never known it to exist, I couldn't ever really attach her memory there. Instead, each day that I looked at the painting, I began to dislike it more. Its depiction of a young woman standing in front of a mirror, dressing for her wedding day, seemed to taunt me.

♦

Before my brother Francis came back into my life, I had already started having a lot of questions about objects and my relationship to them. The opening of a furniture store in lower Manhattan called Totem may have prompted this. Thomas had invested start-up money in the store, and I began to regularly attend the many parties held there. When I asked the owner what Totem meant, he explained that it was an acronym for the objects that evoke meaning.

My questions seemed to spiral from there: At what point does an object have meaning? Is it at the moment you buy it? Or does it have to go through some metamorphosis that alters its state and attaches us to memory in a new way? How exactly does an object evoke meaning?

There is literature on this subject. Jean-Paul Sartre, for example, believed that one reason we desire to have things is in order to enlarge our sense of self. We end up knowing who we are by what we have, he writes, in *Being and Nothingness*. On some level, I must have agreed with this. I had been trying for a long time to define myself mainly through my clothing. Yet the more I had, the less sense of self there seemed to be. Can you enlarge a sense of self, without having fully established that sense to begin with?

For both Francis and me, so many things in the basement of my father's house had meaning. This was confusing. How come some objects could exert such a pull on me and others none at all? Was my sense of identity tied up in my reaction to an object rather than the object itself? If we had stayed in that basement longer, we would have uncovered more artifacts that meant something to us. But what was the strange alchemy that occurred over all those years to give those artifacts such meaning?

I came to the conclusion that my father must have figured that if we wanted anything, we would have claimed it when we had a chance. He had forewarned me that he would sell the house and all its contents to my brother Stephan, and it was his prerogative to do that. Still, I felt he should have understood my distress, the need I had at that moment for him to simply be a father, to make some order of the chaos I felt inside about myself and Francis and the way stacks of old things in a basement could exert such a pull on our hearts and minds. I felt he should have understood that to be set free of such connections could also be perceived as being set adrift.

The emotional pull certain objects had on me came up in other strange ways.

It was also during this time that I began a friendship with a woman named Natalie. We had known each other professionally for several years—she was a fashion fore-caster and I had attended some of her presentations—but we had never been in contact outside of that limited professional sphere. I found her intimidating. She struck me as stern and serious, and as someone who wouldn't take kindly to idle chatter or frivolity. One time I rode in an elevator with her and was too afraid to open my mouth to say hello. She was one of the few people in the fashion world I actually revered.

Somehow, Natalie knew about Thomas's business with trendy electronic products, and she called me to discuss this. We decided to meet at a café on 57th Street, since, coincidentally, she lived down the street from me.

I remember exactly what I wore that day. I wore the rabbit fur tunic that I had purchased at Linda Dresner. I paired this with my slim dark denim Loro Piana jeans, my ankle-length Ralph Lauren boots, and my Fausto Santini bowling bag. My Bulgari sunglasses were perched on top of my head like high-styled antennae picking up signals from who knows where.

Much later, perhaps even several months after that meeting, I realized that this outfit was almost an exact replica of the outfit my mother wore to retrieve me from my early brush with the law — the day I was caught shoplifting at the age of fourteen.

But this is how deep the longing goes. My unconscious self created that outfit. Thomas had always wanted to buy me a fur coat, and I never allowed it. Still, the day I saw that tunic in the Linda Dresner boutique on Park Avenue, I felt compelled to have it. So there I was in that rabbit fur tunic...mimicking the disgraceful chubby...the long tunnel again coming into view. It was impossible to deny.

The day I wore that outfit to meet Natalie, we spent more than three hours talking. We discussed everything from fashion to life on Mars. She turned out to be nothing like I imagined. I understood that my intimidation had only to do with me. Natalie was direct; she looked me in the eyes when we spoke, and she questioned me on things. She was insightful and used her instincts, and this is what I had found intimidating.

Maybe rightfully so. During our conversation, she wasn't content to let me get away with saying anything that I couldn't support. She questioned me in a way that forced me to be honest. Even in a simple conversation, she was looking for the authentic in me. The same thing I had started to search for within myself.

I liked this. I was also scared to death by it.

Eight

MADAME BOVARY
SYNDROME

❧✦❧

In July 2001, the London *Independent* newspaper featured an article about young women who lived loan-filled lifestyles in order to be fashionable, avoid boredom, and bolster their feelings of self-worth. The article named it Madame Bovary syndrome, after Flaubert's tragic literary heroine, whose own boredom and desire for a more grandiose life led her to reckless affairs and overspending.

Was I really like Flaubert's flawed heroine?

At the start of 2001, although not in debt, some of my shopping habits remained erratic and unpredictable. And I was unhappy. Along with this, just like Madame Bovary, I had embarked on an affair. Even so, I didn't feel nearly as much like Madame Bovary as I felt like Wharton's doomed Lily Bart. Like Bart, I had lost my mother and I had refused to marry.

The fact that I hadn't married seemed to be the most salient feature around which my future woes would play out.

I had not secured a financial future for myself, and I would not be able to continue to live in the style I had become accustomed to.

"You blew it," were my father's immortal words when he found out what I had done. I didn't have the nerve to ask if he meant my mistake was not having married Thomas or having the affair. Along with this came a litany of verbal jabs from the boyfriends and husbands of our friends. Certain girlfriends had started out being supportive but eventually pulled away. Like Lily Bart, I was finding out that I had gone out of the bounds of the accepted social norms.

I found myself running around nightclubs with my new boyfriend, a Russian mathematician named Nicholas. He was ten years younger than I and looked it. He seemed to have a perpetually mischievous look in his eye and a child-like grin. He worked in finance but was nothing like the other bankers I had come to know. Nicholas didn't care about fashion or status symbols or impressing me with expensive presents. If there was one thing he enjoyed gifting me with, it was books—titles he insisted I *had* to read.

It's easy to see in hindsight that my initial attraction to Nicholas fell along the same fault lines as my previous relationships. There was drama, impulsiveness, and urgency. My desire to escape the stultifying perfect world I had created was so strong that I ran toward the opposite of it.

So as my decade-long relationship with Thomas unraveled, I could be found jumping up and down at a Romanian dance hall, dancing to the music of a Gypsy punk band, or stumbling through the front door of the speakeasy Milk &

Honey at 3 a.m. I was being carded at Lower East Side beer halls by young men I was old enough to have mothered, and I was waking up at Nick's apartment with blotchy skin and bags under my eyes.

Every day, I regretted ending the relationship with Thomas. Thomas had always been kind, loving, and generous. But what I had begun to realize was this: while Thomas seemed to enjoy the lifestyle, the shopping, and the objects we surrounded ourselves with, I did not. Paradoxically, I both loved the shopping and had started to loathe it. I believe Thomas did not shop to fill any emptiness he felt inside. I did.

I realized that leaving Thomas might be a wrong step, but somewhere in my deepest self was the sense that it was a wrong step in the right direction.

The only question on my mind was *Where do I go from here?* I went to Paris.

By the close of February 2001, I was ensconced in a tiny furnished studio on Rue Saint Martin, with my laptop and a suitcase of winter clothing. The apartment was a bargain at $800 a month, and from Paris I could continue to do most of my magazine work. I had ended the relationship with Nicholas and was talking to Thomas every day. There was a strong possibility that he would come to Paris for the Easter weekend. I kept myself occupied with an extensive essay about fashion photography, and on occasion, I saw the few friends I had in Paris.

And of course, what I did next was decide to go shopping. I decided to go shopping because spring was coming, because I wanted something new to wear when Thomas came, because I felt full of hope for my new life and the new self, who now seemed within reach since I had done something dramatic to bring her to the surface. Maybe now Thomas would understand me; maybe I would finally want to get married and start a family. Maybe the pale blue cotton dress that was hanging on the rack would set the whole rest of my life in motion. I decided to go shopping because I was lonely, sad, and still filled with more uncertainty than ever.

A week before Easter, Thomas called as he had made a habit of doing, exactly at 3 p.m. Paris time, 9 a.m. New York time. Immediately, I detected a distance in his voice, a strain that hadn't been there before. "What's wrong?" I asked.

He hesitated, and with that pause, I knew I was correct.

"I've met someone else," he said.

He refused to give me much detail. He only said he had met her at a dinner party at the home of one of my friends, Carol. He said he thought it might be serious. "I don't think I'm coming to Paris after all. I've been invited to Saint Bart's for Easter," he informed me.

"So you've made your choice?" I asked.

He said, "I think so."

I felt the world drop out from under my feet, but I knew that this was a fair reward for having torn Thomas's world apart. I had broken up that relationship on more than one occasion and had no fair explanation to either him or myself. I had retreated to Paris and asked him to put his life on hold while I tried to figure things out. A logical part of me understood what was happening and why. The other part of me went to bed and couldn't get up for three days.

Eventually, I got out of bed and resumed my Paris life. I unfurled myself from my cocoon slowly, carefully. The first day I managed to buy some food and sit up straight for a few hours. Later, I began to go out to a café or visit the bookshop at the Centre Pompidou. Eventually, I began to work on the essay about fashion photography, which had a fast-approaching deadline. Finally, I began to feel that I needed to do things to improve my appearance. If I could manage that, half the battle would be won. I indulged in almost daily purchases of face creams, eye serums, shampoos, glosses, and anything that promised to exfoliate, resurface, rejuvenate, regenerate, or buff me into a better version of myself. This was not all that new or unusual for me. Back at the apartment in New York, there were three wall cabinets and an entire bathroom cabinet brimming with elixirs and potions that I had amassed over the years. This too had served as part of my shopaholic lifestyle, but I had never acknowledged it as such. It seemed perfectly normal to purchase these items, which could range in cost from a few dollars to several hundred, with little or no thought.

But one day, a few months into my Parisian self-improvement, I cut my foot badly with a cheap callus remover, which was roughly the equivalent of a razor blade with a handle. When I couldn't stem the blood flow, I called a friend to get some advice. "You're not going to like this," he said, certain that he knew me well enough to make such a declaration.

"But the best thing you can do is pour salt in the wound. That will stop the bleeding." I asked if it was going to hurt. He laughed and answered, "Of course, it will hurt."

I hung up the phone and sat at the edge of the tub with my box of salt in one hand and my bloody foot in the other. I poured. It hurt. I started to cry as I watched the blood miraculously begin to coagulate beneath the small mound of white crystals.

Back in New York, Thomas continued his new relationship. In one of our phone conversations, he informed me that he was spending more time at her SoHo loft and less at our old apartment on 56th Street. But, in the same conversation, there would be talk of what it might be like to get back together. It was confusing.

We spoke about former friends, and he fed me crumbs of gossip. He mentioned details about the house at the beach: a woodpecker had made its home in the chimney; the bird of paradise in the lounge had finally died. That house still contained so many things that belonged to me. *How were they? How were my things?* I wanted to ask. It was hard to imagine him there with someone else. His new girlfriend was now there almost every weekend. It was hard to imagine another woman sleeping in the Royalton bed that we had had custom made for our bedroom, another woman loading the dishwasher, sitting on the terrace, swimming in the pool.

Somehow, in the few short months between my affair

and my living in Paris, I had lost the thread of my original intention. I knew it had existed and was certain that it had been substantial enough to warrant my wrong move in the right direction. However, by early summer, there was no direction evident. I simply felt confused. I was living out of a suitcase in a tiny apartment in Paris, holding out hope for a relationship that I wasn't even sure I wanted. I was start- ing to worry about my finances, how much money I needed to live. Would I have to stay in Paris in the tiny apartment? Would I be able to move back to New York?

◆ ◆ ◆

Eventually, there was a trip to New York in early September. I had planned to stay a week. It was nearing six months that I had been living in Paris, trying to get in touch with the me I had avoided for more than a decade, and the trip was supposed to help me in that endeavor. I was hoping to finally answer important questions: Where did I belong? Could I afford to move back to New York? Was the relationship with Thomas finally, definitively over? And where did Nicholas fit into the picture? We were no longer in a relationship, but he had agreed to pick me up at the airport upon my arrival.

As we sped along the East Side Highway in his convert- ible, I felt lighthearted and free. Nicholas said he had tickets to see Jamiroquai at Hammerstein Ballroom the following night and would I like to go? I agreed. In that moment, I felt confident that everything would fall into place.

My second night in New York, I didn't go out at all.

Jet-lagged, I fell asleep by ten o'clock. Of course, I woke around 4 a.m., wide-eyed and jacked up. I remember feeling disoriented, not realizing I was no longer in Paris. That bedroom had always been very dark. It took me a moment to get my bearings. I lay there with my eyes adjusting to the darkness, looking straight ahead at the wall of closets where Thomas had always kept his clothing. Suddenly, I was overcome with the urge to open his closet. Why, I couldn't say. But the desire was strong enough to make me rise from bed, turn on the bedroom light, and pull open the levered doors. That's when I discovered the closets had been completely emptied.

I stood before the great yawning cavity of a closet. Nothing of his remained. Not a single hanger.

I must have believed that as long as his clothing remained in the closet, a part of him was still there. I monitored Thomas's presence in my life based on this fact: his clothing was still in the closet. Looking into the abyss of the empty closet left me hollow. Instinctively, I went to his bathroom and swung open one door of the medicine cabinets, then another, and then another. They had been emptied as well. Two were completely bare, and one contained a jar of skin cream I had never seen before. More than any words that had been spoken, the act of removing his things from what had been our apartment signaled finality.

On September 11, the Twin Towers fell. My plans for returning to Paris were put on hold.

Somewhere in the days that followed, both Mayor Giuliani and President Bush spoke to the public about the disaster, and both expounded on the virtues of shopping in a time of crisis. Shopping, they suggested, was patriotic. It was good for the economy. It was an activity that would help people regain a sense of normalcy. Wasn't that what I had been doing almost all my adult life? Hadn't that been exactly what I had done to regain normalcy after my mother's death?

Still, it struck me as a peculiar prescription in a moment of unprecedented destruction. Go shopping! Is that what we had become as a nation?

Buying is much more American than thinking.

This was one time when I didn't feel like shopping.

At first, I didn't even feel fear. I remember feeling numb. In fact, it wasn't until the anthrax attacks had started several weeks later that I began to feel any emotion, because that was the first time it occurred to me that I was alone. Thomas had retreated to Long Island with his new girlfriend. Nick called me from time to time, but we hardly saw each other. I had been holed up for days in my apartment watching CNN and NY1 and trying to decide if it was safe or practical for me to return to Paris. I had also become ill with something that seemed to be the flu.

When I finally ventured out after three days, it was to go to Bergdorf Goodman to get my hair cut and colored. This was the only thing I could muster the courage or energy to do under the circumstances.

It was a blustery, sunny day, as all of them seemed to be during that time. They seemed to be repeating themselves, blue skies now marred by the sense that something terrible could fall from them in a flash.

As I walked along 57th Street, I saw Nick lumbering toward me, cigarette in hand, silly grin spreading across his face once he spotted me. We stopped in front of each other, and he gave me a quick peck on the lips. He explained that he was on his way to buy a new mobile phone. The night before in some bar or another, he had lost his phone. In between drags on his cigarette, he looked at me critically, tilting his head to one side as he often did when analyzing a situation.

"Something's off," he said, as he blew another circle of smoke into the air.

"What do you mean something's off?" I whimpered.

"You just don't look right. I don't know. You just look... you look like something's off."

"I haven't eaten for three days. Maybe that's what's off."

"Anyway," he said, and he shuffled his feet as he always did when he was either impatient or felt cornered.

"Anyway, what? You seem to want to say something."

"Well, it's just that... with all this stuff going on..." His words trailed off.

"All what stuff?"

"It's just that..."

"Are you breaking up with me?" I asked, but it was a ridiculous question and I half chuckled as I said it. Given the nature of our relationship—on again, off again, me living in Paris—there was no relationship to really break up. Still, I felt he was trying to confirm that he wasn't my boyfriend and couldn't be responsible for me, and this drove home the point that I was on my own.

Nick insisted that he had to run and would call me as he threw the stub of his cigarette into the gutter. He shuffled off, and I was left standing in the street amid the Sturm und Drang of Midtown traffic on that warm, windy afternoon.

While others made plans to leave New York City and never return, I decided that I needed to stay. Even though there was an apartment waiting for me back in Paris, with rent already paid through October, I asked a friend in Paris, who had an extra set of keys, to gather up the few possessions I had left behind and store them until I returned. I would forfeit the remainder of my month's rent and was certain the owner would understand given the circumstance. I never returned to that apartment again. New York was where I needed to be. It didn't make sense for me to run away to a place that wasn't holding any promise. As much as I enjoyed being in Paris, most of my time there had been spent wishing I were back in New York.

The truth was, I was completely unstable. I was like a boat bobbing around on the waves and in desperate need of a safe harbor.

I never went back to the house in the Hamptons. I never went back to the apartment in Paris. I looked in the closet and discovered the clothes were gone. There was a feeling, like a punch in the gut, and there was a *whooshing* sound in my head, like the sound something makes when all its oxygen is sucked away. A vacuum was created. All the air had been forced out of me. I looked in the medicine cabinet and that too was empty except for a jar of face cream that I had never seen before. It was Sisley Global cream. I went to Saks the next morning and walked over to the Sisley counter.

"Do you have the Global cream?" I asked the woman who stood behind a display of jars and tubes of various shapes and sizes. She placed the tips of her perfectly manicured fingers over one short cylindrically shaped glass. I immediately recognized the jar as being the same one that had mysteriously appeared in the cabinet.

"How much?" I asked.

"Two hundred and eighty dollars," she answered.

And so I left Saks Fifth Avenue that day with a jar of Sisley Global face cream, which cost more than a year's worth of Time Warner Cable, more than half a year's grocery bill, roughly a quarter of the price of a new laptop computer (which would have been one thing I could have benefited from). I needed to concentrate on my work and on my financial health and on figuring out how I was going to live. Things were changing on an almost daily basis; the world seemed to be turned upside down. The security of a man, my usual fallback, was nowhere in sight, and New York was in a choke hold of fear and uncertainty. So what in the world could a jar of Sisley Global face cream do for me at a time like that?

Nine

START WHERE YOU LEFT OFF . . . DO NOT AVOID THE DIFFICULT PARTS

※※

One day, I felt the need to take inventory of things found in the back of my closet. What I found was this: A Jil Sander latte-colored cashmere blanket coat, moth infested, half a lapel eaten away. An Agnès B. cream-colored polo sweater bought at their SoHo store, sensible, classic, short sleeved, round neck—never worn, price tag still attached. A pair of Giorgio Armani alligator-skin driving shoes a half size too small, worn once with a caramel-colored Armani viscose and wool double-breasted pants suit, and now sorely out of style. A daisy chain of bras—Eres, La Perla, Calvin Klein, French lace, pale pink and sprigged with wildflowers, a saucy striped balconette. A Prada dress—black, three-quarter sleeves with a pencil-cut skirt, hit just below the knee, impossible to walk in, worn to Lisa's wedding with putty-colored suede sandals from Costume

National. A Christian Lacroix multilayered tulle ballerina skirt the color of cheap ballpoint ink—large, unwieldy, and refusing to yield to doorways. Purchased in a moment of utter madness, no doubt.

In the spring of 2002, I decided to take a trip to Belize in Central America. It would be the second time I was traveling to Belize. The first time had been over a decade earlier. It was one of the first trips I had ever taken with Thomas. We had stayed in a luxurious inn on the Ambergris Key and had gone scuba diving and snorkeling during the day and done the romantic candlelight dinner thing by night.

There is a photograph of me during that trip. I am wearing a black spandex minidress with silver buckles on the shoulder straps. My feet are bare, but I am wearing an Ebel diving watch. It was the first watch Thomas had bought for me.

I knew this second trip to Belize would be nothing like the first trip. It would be different because I was different. Somewhere in my mind, I categorized it as a chance to get things right.

Start where you left off; do not avoid the difficult parts. Those were the words that were written on a tiny white strip of paper nestled inside a fortune cookie. I had kept the message with me over the past two years. It had been taped to the refrigerator at the apartment in Paris. I had carried it in my agenda.

♦

So this was both an escape from shopping and a place where shopping provided no escape. Aside from the local bodega or roadside vendors hawking local crafts, shopping in Belize was nonexistent. And that was a good thing. I hadn't come back to Central America to continue to buy my way into oblivion.

It was just the opposite. I had come to the tiny Central American country with the hope of rediscovering something I used to love about myself: I had once been an avid scuba diver. This trip was to be one week in the jungle, the interior, and then a week out on the keys to go diving along the great reef and the famous Blue Hole.

The first week in the jungle was roughing it. It had nothing to do with creature comforts. I stayed in a ten-dollar-a-night communal camp and slept in a mud hut; I showered outdoors beneath a bucket of cold rainwater. The first evening I fell asleep to the sound of distant animal cries, and the first morning I woke to find a tarantula in my bed.

At dinner, I realized that the opposite wasn't as easy to navigate as I had hoped. Most of the other guests were at least a decade younger than me. I felt uncomfortable, silly, and too old to be talking about having to hide my stash of pot from Mom or reminiscing about spring break. It aggravated me, the way everyone seemed jazzed about their trip and the caving they were going to do. Belize, famous for its network of limestone caves, had begun to attract more of these novice adventurers and ecotourists.

Luckily, there was one guide who offered to take me and another guest on a private tour of one of the caves. As the deal was negotiated, I cataloged my reasons for wanting to do such a thing.

Going in a cave seemed metaphorically correct. It was partly about hiding, partly about turning off the noise of the world to discover myself, but mostly it was about going deeper. So much of my unhappiness in my life with Thomas stemmed from tuning myself out. I was so trapped in the lacquer of the good life, I had acknowledged neither my real emotions nor my desires.

I knew when I left that lifestyle that one of my goals was to be reacquainted with myself, to become aware of the emotions that I had managed to turn off for more than a decade. And so going closer to the center of the earth seemed an apt metaphor for going to the center of myself. I wanted to learn about myself again. What was I capable of? Where were my physical limitations? At least this is what I was trying to tell myself as we set out the next morning toward a place ominously named Wonderland.

Our guide, whose name was Abel, was left-handed. I noticed this as he sliced through the jungle overgrowth with his machete while leading us up a dirt path on the way to the cave. "It's no longer open to the public," he explained, as we climbed higher. I could barely hear his voice rise from the back of his head. "But I think it's one of the most beautiful caves to see."

He turned around to look at me. "Are you okay?"

"Yes. So far, so good," I answered.

Truth was, I was nervous as hell. I hadn't challenged myself physically in years. I wasn't sure I was up to the task.

When we finally arrived at the mouth of the cave, we sat down on a level rock and ate some sandwiches that Abel had prepared. "It's good to go in with energy," he explained.

After lunch, I watched closely as he began to unload gear from his backpack. He pulled out flashlights and backup batteries, some colorful ropes, helmets, and gloves. As I watched him, I looked for signs of competence, something to reassure me he could be completely trusted. After all, I was allowing myself to go down into a hole in the earth to be led around a labyrinth of dark tunnels with this man. His reassuring name was not enough. I looked for signs to calm myself. When I saw him foraging around in his backpack, I got the sense something was wrong.

"What is it?" I asked anxiously.

"I think I've forgotten the rope ladder," he said without lifting his head to look at me.

I wanted to turn back, but he convinced me we should go ahead. The rope ladder wouldn't really be critical until the end of the trip, when we left the cave, he explained. He thought we could improvise.

I wasn't comfortable with this situation. After all, I was the weak link in the team, the girl with the inferior upper-body strength. Still, I didn't want to disappoint them. We had hiked a long way already. Also, I didn't want to disappoint myself. I wanted to complete the journey and prove that I could do it.

And so I allowed myself to be lowered down the wall into the cave. I landed on a narrow ledge and waited for the others. I had on my hat with the searchlight and my new sneakers.

When I managed to get my bearings, I looked around. The cave was already magnificent, and we hadn't even reached the part that was called Wonderland. It was filled with abundant stalactites that hung high overhead, like the spirals of a great cathedral, dangling upside down. They looked like sugar candy.

Abel led us along the ledge that sometimes narrowed to a dangerous sliver. We went deeper and it got darker. We stopped and turned off our headlamps to experience the complete darkness. I had never before been in such darkness and it both frightened and exhilarated me. But after a while, I could feel myself getting colder, fatigued.

I asked if we could stop and rest again. All three of us knelt, backs against a cool wall of rock, and looked out into the dazzling view: an entire skyline of stalactite spirals that were more intricate and beautiful than anything I'd ever seen.

"You have this," I said to Abel. "You really don't need to go to Manhattan."

We stood up and continued farther, walking gingerly along the narrow ledges, stopping at various points to take in the view, but I was beginning to feel very cold now and very exhausted. At one point, I felt I had to stop.

"I can't go any farther," I declared. "I'm not going to make it to Wonderland."

They looked unhappy, but there must have been

something about my appearance that made them both agree. "Okay," Abel said, and he placed a reassuring hand on my shoulder. "We'll turn around now."

I got the feeling he was worried about the exit. We still had to navigate getting me out, up the steep wall without the rope ladder. Abel must have sensed that it would be impossible for me if I became too physically drained.

The walk back seemed shorter and less treacherous, and for a moment I was afraid I had bailed out too soon. I should have tried to make it all the way. However, when we reached that wall, I was convinced I had done the right thing. It was practically vertical, at least fifteen feet high. I would have to try to climb out.

Abel climbed up first and tried to show me where to get a grip and anchor my feet. I watched intensely, but my first attempt failed. When I realized I didn't have the upper-body strength to hold on, I felt a wave of panic. The other hiker offered another suggestion. If I tried to straddle the opposite wall on the way up, I could rely more on the strength in my legs. The only problem with that was that if I fell it meant a drop into a crevice. I remember trying to make light of things, crack a joke. But I could feel my heart beating in my chest, and my palms were coated in sweat.

And yet I felt exhilarated and challenged, and more alive than I had been in years.

I took a moment to breathe deeply; I wiped my sweaty hands on my trousers.

I took the advice and started up the back wall. Halfway up, I had to stretch one leg out onto the facing wall and make a lunge. I took a deep breath and leaped forward and secured my foot into a small indentation. I located the small ledge where Abel had instructed me to place my hands and reached out to grab it. At that point, I knew I would make it the rest of the way. A few seconds later, I was out of the cave.

After spending a week in the jungle, I traveled to the sea, out to Ambergris Key. I would finally get to do some diving. I had not been diving for more than a decade and felt a nagging urgency to be underwater again.

The last time I had been diving was also in Belize, and it was with Thomas. We had gone out on a boat with a dive master and a few other enthusiasts. Thomas, who had no real diving experience (he had learned the basics in a swimming pool in Manhattan), geared up and jumped off the back of the boat in a hurry, perhaps to show off a little. In no time he was being carried away by the current and flailing his arms. The dive master had to swim out to save him. After that, we never went diving again. The story of the failed dive trip was often repeated to friends who laughed hysterically.

This time wasn't much different: same location. As the boat pulled out of the slip, I noticed its name, *Comfortably Numb,* and that made me laugh.

Jumping into the water was like a rebirth. I let the bracing ocean water trickle under the skin of my wet suit and felt it being warmed by my own body temperature. I was surprised at how familiar this was. I recalled having had the same sensation when I went on a dive trip not long after my mother died. It was in Florida, an outing on a small boat.

That time as well I had jumped into the sea and had the strongest sense of my own aliveness—the vibrancy of my own existence startling me.

By the end of the trip, I felt I was doing things for me again, things I had remembered liking. The adventurer in me had come back. Shopping seemed like something in the distance. I could take it or leave it.

When I returned to New York, I realized that people had started to relate to me differently. No longer part of the Hamptons world, my relationships with most of my former friends from there were strained, if not finished. It seems that all the clout I had from living in the large white house with Thomas had evaporated. My coach had turned into a pumpkin. Now, to go to the Hamptons meant being invited to someone's beach house on one of those very hot, sticky New York summer weekends.

These invites were hardly forthcoming, and I'm certain I would not have accepted most had they suddenly materialized. I didn't have any real desire to go there.

The only invitation I did accept was from my friend Rosanne, and that was based on my desire to spend some time with her more than wanting to be anywhere near the beach. Rosanne was a single, successful financial analyst who always left me with the impression that she was working too hard and traveling too often. She was one of the few friends who didn't judge my departure from Thomas harshly.

She seemed to have accepted my decision without question or criticism.

So one Saturday morning, we drove out to the beach, along the familiar landscape of the Long Island Expressway. The drive itself made me sentimental, something I hadn't expected.

As we approached Southampton town, she suggested we stop at the market to pick up some groceries. "If you don't mind, I just want to stop in Cashmere Hampton to get some sweaters," she added.

"Sure," I said. "That would be great."

Rosanne parked the car, and as she did, I started to feel the emotional weight of what I was doing. The weekend felt like a monumental mistake; I wanted to turn around and go back home. *Please, just put me on the bus, and let me go home.*

When I walked into the Cashmere Hampton boutique, I felt lost. I could no longer afford to buy myself expensive cashmere sweaters and almost didn't know what to do with myself in the confines of the shop. As Rosanne tried on cardigans and zip-front hoodies, I pawed through some sweaters folded on a display table and felt like my chest was going to burst open. I had not anticipated feeling so much emotion about being back in the Hamptons. I hadn't anticipated having to encounter that familiar shopping terrain, the places I used to shop.

It would have been the perfect time to buy myself something—an act that had so often eased emotional pain—but none of my credit cards would be accepted at that point, and I barely had enough cash to pay for myself over the course of the weekend.

I advised Rosanne on which sweaters to buy and watched as the shopkeeper bagged her purchase. I left the shop with a small razor-toothed sweater brush that was a gift from the shopkeeper. Rosanne left with a bag bulging with new things to wear.

That weekend I felt a sharp delineation between my former life and the one I now lived. To be in the Hamptons as only an invited guest, as a person who truly couldn't afford to be there, was my new designation. I had not given this fact much thought; I must have been too busy trying to get my life in order. Status had never been what I was chasing after. Yet the situation left me feeling diminished. If no longer the lady of any house, no longer someone who could afford to even buy a cashmere sweater, who was I?

Rosanne and I navigated the rest of that weekend carefully. We spent a lot of time at her house, cooked and talked and went to see a movie. At no point during that trip did I want to talk about old times spent in that house, but they just seemed to be hanging in the air, as old times sometimes do. I told Rosanne that in all the years I had been coming to that house — for summer weekends, for tennis games, for the annual paella on New Year's Eve — I had never once gone upstairs to the bedrooms. I had been in the basement to play pool, I had been in the swimming pool, and I had even managed to land on the tennis court a few times, even though I didn't play tennis. Yet not once had I ever treaded up the single flight of stairs to even glance at the bedrooms. "It feels strange to now be sleeping in one of them," I said.

I was trying to be stoic during this time and imagined myself with a facial expression like an explorer squinting out over an expansive sea. My future, like a welcome patch of land, was nowhere in sight, and yet I had to maintain a posture of expectation and confidence. And so I displayed this posture when I told Rosanne about a guy I had started dating. His name was Jason, I said. But I stopped short of telling her that I found him to be terrifically boring and self-centered. I sugarcoated him for her benefit or perhaps for my own.

"Does he have money?" she asked.

"Well, yes," I confided. "He's only forty, and he's already retired."

"Marry him!" she answered without blinking an eye.

The precariousness of my situation was obvious to almost everyone but me. Thomas bought me a book titled *Courage* and wrote on the inside cover, "Somehow this made me think of you." What did he mean by that? Did he mean he thought me courageous? Or did he mean I would need a lot of courage to face a future without him?

I wasn't feeling courageous, but I was starting to feel concerned.

The next thing I needed to do was find a new apartment. I would have to leave the two-bedroom apartment; the lease was ending. It was clear that I was in no position to take over a rent that would be veering close to $4,000 a month. As much as I wanted to stay in the comfort, luxury, and familiarity of my spacious apartment, it was no longer part of my lifestyle.

One afternoon I had to take refuge in Club Monaco on lower Fifth Avenue. I had just come from viewing an apartment — a sunny one bedroom on Mott Street that was going for $1,600 a month — when I realized my application probably wouldn't be approved. The apartment was in the neighborhood that I loved. It was on the same street as Cafe Gitane and just around the corner from Nicholas's old apartment, and in my mind it would be the perfect neighborhood in which I could embark on my new life. That neighborhood appeared to fulfill every fantasy of the me I wanted to become in the wake of my split from Thomas. I pictured myself sitting in Cafe Gitane, buying overpriced almond croissants at the French bakery, or shopping for lingerie at the fancy little boutique just down the street.

Yes, there I was making up magazine-style pictures of my life again.

The reality was quite different. I needed a cosigner, a guarantor for the rent. My freelance salary wasn't enough to satisfy the most lenient of landlords, and my credit rating had started to slide. These realities were now coming home to roost. No lease could be signed without a guarantor.

Still, instead of doing something about my situation, I was in Club Monaco, looking through the sale rack, when the phone rang. It was Thomas. I had called him and asked if he'd help me to secure a smaller apartment in the same building where we had lived.

He said he would.

Thomas agreed to sign as a guarantor on the first year's lease. After that, I would be on my own. I convinced myself that in that year I would manage to make enough money to pay the rent, make my credit card payments, and continue to shop.

I managed to get the studio apartment on the twenty-second floor that overlooked the Hudson River and, coincidentally, the windowless building where my father had worked for almost thirty years. The view was critical to me because the apartment was so small. Without the view, it would feel sad, depressing, and claustrophobic. I ended up giving Thomas all of the old furniture to place in storage for me: the couch, a glass coffee table, an Italian bookcase, two side chairs, an end table, various kitchen appliances. None of it would fit in the new place.

What was left was crammed into the tiny, new apartment. The Fortuny lamp that once seemed too small now loomed over the bed. The steel and leather bench that had been in the foyer was now wedged just in front of the closet. Below it, I stashed all my magazines, another component of my shopping habit. I could not stop buying magazines.

The bookshelves that had been custom built to fit in the large master bedroom, which had served as my office, were clustered against the north-facing wall. They fit perfectly but without an inch to spare.

Finally, my desk, which had already been traveling with me for more than a decade, was placed in front of the expanse of windows. The closets, thankfully, were abundant: There were four in total. And for a small apartment, they were miraculously ample. I managed to get my entire wardrobe, including all my shoes, in them without any overflow.

Then there was the arrival of Warren.

My friend Alexandra suggested we meet. He was a photography collector. I had started to write more about photography.

Even though I didn't like the way he had one button too many open on his shirt, I flirted with him over lunch at Cipriani. I flirted, and I tried to impress him with my knowledge of photography. He was a serious collector and a philanthropist who contributed generously to some of New York's most prestigious museums. And so I mentioned the growing interest in Chinese photographers and the astronomical prices some images were commanding at auction. We agreed that it was "funny money" fueling that market, and I felt content that I had impressed him. But I was also keenly aware that I was playing a role, disguising myself in a froth of what I felt I should be, say, and do.

After all, this was a blind date, and that's what I was supposed to do. I knew how to flirt with him because he reminded me so much of Thomas. He too was European, and he was blond, and he was wealthy. I knew that was at least part of the reason I was sitting across a table from him that day, watching the way the sun moved across the white starched tablecloth, stirring my iced tea too slowly, smiling into the distance when he said something thought provoking, and cracking the occasional smart remark in order to display my wit. At the time, the consensus among my friends was that a rich man made as good a boyfriend as any. So when he asked to see me again, I said yes.

For my second date with Warren, I deliberately showed up at his Fifth Avenue apartment wearing something conservative and proper, if not downright dowdy. As I was dressing, I remember being conscious of trying to construct an outfit that wouldn't rattle any Upper East Side nerves. I must have been carrying this image over from the Hamptons, of all those Stepford-looking women with the same lemony blond highlights in their hair, the same Tod's loafers, twinsets, and sensible slacks.

So there I was, in costume, arriving at Warren's, being announced by the concierge with the white gloves and the fancy hat. I stood in the lobby trying to look like I belonged there. I rode up in the elevator making polite conversation with the friendly operator.

As the elevator's metal cage door opened, Warren appeared in the foyer. He wore a white linen button-down shirt with the sleeves rolled halfway up his arms. Beneath this, he had on a navy blue block-print sarong.

I was completely destabilized by this outfit.

Suddenly, I felt unnaturally prim in my high-necked knit sweater and floaty floral skirt. What had I been thinking? Who was I trying to look like? Maybe I didn't know how to do the rich guy thing after all. Maybe I didn't really want to.

Warren showed me around the apartment that was as large as a gymnasium with a wraparound porch that overlooked Central Park. I stayed outside on the porch while he went into his bedroom to change his clothing. He came back wearing a pair of loose linen trousers and leather sandals. He looked so relaxed and natural. We went to dinner, and the entire time I felt like a woman in the wrong skin.

A few weeks later, after we finished a lunch date, Warren asked the taxi driver to pull over in front of the Issey Miyake boutique on Madison Avenue. "There's a handbag in here I thought you might like," he said, as he opened the door and stepped onto the sidewalk.

The next thing I knew we were inside the shop, and Warren was handing me a pair of steel gray iridescent trousers that looked like they were modeled after the kind of pants astronauts wore.

"Here, try these," he said. As I took the pants in my hands and headed toward the curtained cubicle, he grabbed a glittery T-shirt and a boxy black jacket. "Here, try these too," he insisted.

I stood in the cubicle and checked the price tag on the T-shirt. It was seven hundred dollars. "Oh, no," I whispered. "Not this." I had to be careful; I did not want to fall into a relationship with a wealthy man who might think my affections could be bought.

A minute later, I stepped out of the cubicle and spun around like a mannequin. Everyone *oohed* and *aahed*. Then I quickly disappeared back into the dressing cubicle. As I was struggling to lace up my boots, Warren pushed the curtain aside and grabbed all three items that I had just modeled. I protested. "Hey, wait a minute—"

Fully dressed again, I emerged from behind the curtain to find a salesgirl handing me a bulging, oversized Issey Miyake shopping bag. "The purse I thought you might like is in there too," Warren said.

He escorted me out of the store with a hand on the small of my back and ushered me into the plush environment of the waiting car.

As we sped down Park Avenue, he asked where I'd like to be dropped off.

I was deposited on the corner of 57th Street and Park Avenue, shopping bag in hand, and Warren drove quickly out of sight.

I had been on enough shopping excursions with men to know that there probably were strings attached, and for a woman, like myself, who was trying to keep up appearances, the seductive pull of those strings was strong. But I also knew I didn't want to be treading those murky waters. It would have been easy to let myself be taken in, to be bought. And yet the situation left me feeling sad.

When I wore the new Issey Miyake pants and T-shirt to Warren's birthday dinner, I can't say that sadness dominated the evening. I liked the way I looked in that outfit and knew that my confidence was boosted wearing it. At the restaurant in Union Square, I waltzed to the ladies room with a sense of ease, aware of the attention the new clothing attracted.

But I can't say I didn't feel uneasy wearing that outfit either.

After dinner, Warren dropped me off in front of my apartment building. There was confusion and utter clarity in this moment. I wasn't in love with Warren and knew that I could never be in love him.

And I never allowed Warren to take me shopping again.

Start where you left off . . . do not avoid the difficult parts.

That was the fortune I uncovered in a Chinese fortune cookie at downtown's Peking Duck House back in early 2001. That was the fortune I had tucked into my embossed leather agenda, had taped to the refrigerator in my Paris apartment, and had placed in a black porcelain ashtray that I kept in the far right corner of my desk.

Start where you left off . . . do not avoid the difficult parts. What were the difficult parts? Where had I left off? Obviously, I had kept that tiny piece of paper for a reason. It struck a chord—it seemed uncannily like a psychic reading of who I was. I had spent my life avoiding the difficult parts, running away from them at every possible chance. I now knew my pattern well, could see it in every movie I played in my head of the past. I didn't want to repeat the same mistakes.

It would have been the easiest move in the world to fall into the ether of Warren's rarefied world. Somewhere inside me, I knew that would be the very definition of failure. But the part of me that still wanted to be saved found it hard to resist.

Ten

BETTER TO SHOP
THAN PRAY

※※

I had gotten into the habit of placating myself with small gifts. One day, I went and bought myself a silk camisole with straps thinner than fishing line. The fabric was a leafy print—it reminded me of the negative of a photograph—black, gray, and white. It was spring when I bought that camisole, but I imagined myself wearing it in the summer, maybe with a black satin skirt and high-heeled sandals. I imagined the way I would throw my shoulders back to keep the straps from sliding off them. I imagined walking down the street in this camisole feeling strong and confident and sexy. I pictured myself standing at a street corner, waiting for the light to change. I pictured a man standing across the street, noticing me, but I would remain looking straight ahead, pretending not to notice him. I was preoccupied with the shoulder straps of that camisole and the way they would feel on my skin.

As I walked home with that purchase, I concluded that no matter how much money I earned it would never be enough. I had this sickening inability to manage my finances. This was part of the disorder's delicious undertow. Part of the thrill of each purchase was the very sensation that I was doing something wrong: spending money that I didn't have. Is this what a criminal feels like? Did I want to be caught? Did I want someone to come along and save me, or did I simply want to throw up my hands and cry uncle. Okay, I was found out. Now, please, somebody get me some help.

For all my difficulties, my starts and stops, I had managed to make progress with my magazine writing career. My first article for British *Vogue* was published in June 2002. There I was, a published writer in *Vogue*. And there I was — forever the daughter, forever wanting to wear the gloss of approval — wishing that my mother were alive to see me reach that milestone.

The article was about the artist Philip-Lorca diCorcia, a photographer featured regularly on the pages of *W* magazine. He had become known for his use of narrative, or story lines, in his fashion photography and had just written a new book featuring a collection of personal photographs, with the title *A Storybook Life.*

Telling stories seemed to be the trend. Fantasy was in style. During this time, the stories depicted on the pages of fashion magazines became increasingly elaborate and sometimes audacious. DiCorcia's were singled out for their painterly qualities and theatrical lighting and for the fact that they sometimes appeared to challenge the very values that the fashion magazines endorsed.

I had been warned that he could be an intellectually demanding subject, who was not content to discuss the superficial aspects of his craft. This intrigued rather than intimidated me, and besides, I wanted to do a good job on my first *Vogue* assignment. I wasn't going to let small challenges get in my way.

As things turned out, the interview wasn't that demanding after all. We ended up enjoying a long, animated conversation. This offered a burst of confidence I desperately needed.

A few weeks later when he invited me to a dinner party at his apartment, I happily accepted and found myself in the company of a few other photographers, a Russian magazine editor and ad film producer. There, once again, I felt the seductive pull of the magazine world that I loved. Everyone appeared to be in perpetual motion, constantly taking trips to exotic locales and having fantastic experiences. But spending time around fashion people required a certain kind of stamina; there was the constant need to be on top of things, to know the latest who, what, when, where, and why. As much as I wished to be admitted to this inner sanctum of image makers, I was weary of the velvet rope judgments they sometimes applied.

There was still a long distance between where I was and where I wanted to be. Yes, I had made my way into the pantheon of *Vogue* writers, but that alone was not going to sustain me. Being invited to dinner parties with interesting people from the magazine world might yield some new contacts, but it was not going to make my problems go away.

As much as I was exhilarated by my accomplishments and the independence that represented, I found myself fretting about my appearance. I was wearing an old coat that winter, a Trussardi shearling that was starting to lose its gloss. It desperately needed a cleaning, and the buttons were always coming loose. My cultivated perfection was starting to show signs of wear and tear. In the judgmental magazine world, I was afraid my appearance would start to betray me.

Of course, I wanted to buy a new coat, but I couldn't afford one. I could no longer use any of my credit cards. It seemed only a matter of time before my house of credit cards would come tumbling down. The whole thing was perched on such a precarious limb that it seemed impossible to keep it balanced.

I had stopped looking at my credit card statements some months before and had stopped answering the phone. The calls from collection agencies were almost nonstop, coming at all hours of the morning and late into evening. I had not mastered the art of disguising my voice, and I was not very good at flat-out lies. A few times, I did try to say I wasn't in, but I faltered before the words were even out of my mouth. Being such a lightweight, I actually felt afraid of the debt collector barking at me on the other end of the telephone: "Are you sure she's not in?"

No, I was never too sure of anything those days, and

least of all my ability to either pay or sidestep those pit bulls. Some were remarkably clever (or I was remarkably gullible) and would have me writing something called a "check by phone" for my last twenty dollars. I would write VOID on the check, give the bank the check number, and the bank would electronically remove the funds from my account. There was one caller in particular who had me in tears on more than one occasion. I still tremble just thinking about the timbre of his voice, the absolute certainty with which he could say, "This is what you are going to pay."

On another occasion, a tandem approach, two women on a conference call, got me to do a "check by phone" to the tune of $500. That left me short on my next month's rent. It felt like having a blanket that was always too skimpy—pull it up to cover your shoulders, and then you're left with chilly feet.

It would make sense that this level of discomfort would be matched by a mammoth resolve to set things straight. It might be logical that I would gather my faculties and come up with some master plan to get things in order. But that was never quite the way I approached things during this time. I had no discernible plan, but rather kept hoping that things would get better while I doggedly pursued my writing career. I hung on to small conquests like stars and began to pursue this with a fervor that I hadn't ever shown for my work in the past.

Somehow, within all this madness, I maintained a desire to buy new things for myself. Waking in the middle of the night, racked with fear for my future, I would resolve to get myself under control and to make a dramatic change. But the next day I might find myself on Lexington Avenue just in front of Bloomingdale's. I would have to go inside.

Inevitably, I would end up purchasing silly things. It might be a faux-leather motorcycle jacket or a Juicy Couture terry-cloth tracksuit or a Calvin Klein bra or a new face cream or eye serum. As my financial situation worsened, cosmetics took on a new importance. I was enthralled with cosmeseu-ticals with newfangled names and outrageous promises. I would find myself buying serums, tonics, and lotions that promised to hold back time, springing for these items mostly because they could be had for twenty or thirty dollars a pop.

Sometimes it felt as if I simply needed to remind myself that I was still able to shop. I would duck into Banana Repub-lic and buy three T-shirts only to go through the motions of shopping at Banana Republic. And I would feel alive.

Other times, it was about something I called the miracle factor: the belief that if I purchased a particular item it would change my life. I didn't want to pray for a miracle, I wanted to shop for a miracle. In fact, I wanted to actually be the miracle. And, as usual, I thought the only necessary component of this process was to look the part. The miracle me would have to be wearing something that could allow for the miracle to happen. I had been so tuned in to build-ing myself from the outside that, silly as this may sound, it was ingrained in my thinking process. I believed that cer-tain items of clothing or creating a certain appearance could make things turn out for the better. I wasn't so foolish as to believe that buying things would magically pay my debts.

But I was silly enough to believe that buying the right shoes to wear with that Prada dress would cause a chain reaction of events that could change the course of my life.

While I continued to try to keep everything polished and perfect on the outside, inside I was a cocktail of depression, self-loathing, regret, and fear. The only thing that made me feel worse about myself was more shopping. The only thing that made me feel better about myself was more shopping.

It amazes me how I managed to avoid any dialogue about the way shopping was affecting my life. The issue of personal finances remained taboo. The only one who had any true sense of my predicament was Thomas. At that point, even he was not fully aware of the mess I was creating for myself. Besides, I had been busy, like a hamster in a wheel, keeping up appearances, making sure that I still managed to look the part.

In core fusion class, I would scan the room and see a collection of New York women much like myself. Most were in their thirties or early forties and extremely well groomed. They, like me, appeared to be aiming for perfection. I would watch some of them preen before the mirrors, balance at the ballet bar while waiting for class to commence. Everyone wore expensive stretch pants and cropped tops and had their expensive hair pulled into high, tight ponytails. We all looked similar, like perfect specimens.

And this made me wonder if they too—at least some of

them—suffered from the same problems. Was there someone in that class who had the same compulsive shopping habit? And if so, how would I recognize her? Could it be possible that I was the only one in New York City waking up in a cold sweat at night, wondering how she was going to pay her bills? That hardly seemed possible. Yet when I looked around that room, everyone had the same cool, collected demeanor. But was this just part of the act? Was that what was necessary to survive in New York City? So much was about appearances, not letting your guard down. So much was about looking good rather than actually feeling good, actually being good.

Statistically, with at least 6 percent of the population suspected of having a compulsive shopping disorder, it was more than likely that on any given day I passed someone on the street who had a similarly distorted relationship with shopping, who had trouble prying herself away from the mindless acquisition of objects, or was even wrestling with personal debt.

The subject of personal finances didn't come up often in conversations with my girlfriends, but if it did, I had a knack for avoiding speaking directly about myself. One time, when a friend who owned her own business mentioned that she always told her assistants "one of the most important things they can do for themselves is maintain a good credit rating," I shook my head vigorously in agreement. It would have been the perfect opportunity for me to discuss my own credit card debt, but I was too proud, too frightened, of how this might be perceived.

Although compulsive shopping has since come to be more openly discussed, in 2002, truths about shopping addiction were hardly evident in the media or on the densely populated sidewalks of Manhattan. The vision on the street was that almost everyone was affluent and whole. We had become a society that understood ourselves and others by what we bought, wore, and drove. If anyone had a shopping problem, it was a carefully guarded secret.

Shopping was not supposed to be a problem. Popular wisdom—the kind presented in books, movies, and television shows at the time—was that savvy women found ways to shop. One way was to continue to apply for more credit. Another was to find a rich boyfriend. Like a salmon swimming against the stream, I rejected this option.

A few weeks earlier, I had pulled the plug on my relationship with Warren.

One afternoon as Warren and I shared a plate of oysters at the Sea Grill in Rockefeller Center, he extended an invitation for me to come to Saint Bart's over the Christmas holiday.

"It would be nice," he said simply.

At first, this sounded too good to be true.

"That sounds great," I said, as I leaned over to kiss his cheek, perfectly flecked with a two-day stubble.

"I'll book you a flight," he said. "You can come on the twenty-fifth and leave on the thirtieth," he continued.

"But why leave before New Year's?" I blurted out instinctively without taking the necessary pause — a pause in which I might have understood what was being said. But before my sentence had completely disappeared from the air, I thought I knew why. There would probably be someone else arriving for the time of the New Year. I was invited for slot number one, and she, whoever she may have been, must have already claimed slot number two.

I did not accept the invitation to Saint Bart's. However victorious this was for my self-esteem, it felt like a defeat. Warren went away for the holiday, and I stayed alone in New York. I don't remember that Christmas with any clarity. I want to say that I spent the day in bed, but I know that's what I had done the Christmas before. Was it possible that I had spent two Christmases in a row alone in bed? Yes, it was.

There were women who easily accepted this. I knew some of them. And I saw how they managed to make use of a man's money and status with their endgame in mind or how they excelled in the art of tabling their own emotions. I did not know what the secret was to this methodology, but I had watched some women pull it off.

I knew of one woman who was always hitching herself to high rollers in finance in the style of a rodeo cowgirl. No matter how rough the ride, she managed to hang on. When she was invited to spend Christmas at a castle in England, she accepted, even though she knew it would mean leaving, quite literally, as the clock was striking twelve on December 31, as the next guest was arriving. Instead of being upset, she simply asked to be escorted to the airport and placed on a first-class flight to the nearest ski resort. When she was spotted on the slopes on New Year's Day, she looked no worse for wear, and tongues weren't wagging about her dismissal from the castle. She even accepted his gift, an expensive necklace, and wore it with no regrets for the entirety of the next year.

It was clear I did not have that kind of "game." I didn't have any "game" at all.

♦ ♦ ♦

The promise of a pill. I was searching for an answer, despite the fact that I had yet to properly define my problem. What exactly was my problem? Even though I was having trouble paying my bills, I couldn't stop shopping.

I remembered an article, a brief piece in *Time* magazine, dated December 25, 2000, that referred to the antidepressant Celexa. The article described the drug as a serotonin reuptake inhibitor, a "shopper's little helper," that in medical studies had managed to curb the compulsive behavior of at least a few shoppers. The article ended with the brief derision: "just in time for the holidays."

Even in the media, compulsive shopping disorder was being dismissed as laughable, something that was perhaps a cop-out, not to be taken seriously. Not surprisingly, shopping addiction is often referred to as the "smiled upon" addiction. But I had started to take my compulsive shopping seriously. My strongest desire was to find something to help me cope with the agitation and arousal I experienced during certain shopping episodes, and it seemed Celexa might have something to offer because it worked on serotonin. Serotonin, I knew, was the brain chemical related to migraine headaches. (It is often a sharp dip in serotonin levels that signals the onset of a migraine.) I have suffered from migraines since my early twenties. The serotonin connection felt like a sign: perhaps my migraines and my strange shopping episodes were in some way related.

I decided to try Celexa and secured a sample from a doctor friend of a friend.

A few weeks later, I stood in the bathroom and popped the little pink pill from its blister pack. I swallowed it with a glass of water and went about my usual day.

However, on the drug, I experienced nothing more than a kind of mild creative paralysis. Within a few hours of taking the first dose, I felt dulled. I couldn't get a thought straight or string an original sentence together. I felt spacey, untethered, and unable to focus. Clearly, I was just a pushover for anything that is written up on the pages of a glossy magazine.

My episode with Celexa left me with more questions than answers. Was my shopping problem nature or nurture? Character or chemistry? Did I have a biology predisposed to compulsive behavior? Would trying to fine-tune myself with drugs be a possible cure?

In fact, it turns out that there are distinct brain patterns associated with shopping.

I now know, thanks to a group of researchers at Stanford University, that when I want to make a purchase, there is an increased flow of oxygen-rich blood to an area of my brain known as the nucleus accumbens. In addition, I also know, according to another group of researchers at MIT, that the brain has distinct circuits for registering that you want something or recoiling at the price. And I know that the price of a product can influence something known as "experienced pleasantness," which may cause me to enjoy something more simply because it is more expensive.

I know this, because I've read it in myriad newspaper and magazine articles. Still, as curious as this burgeoning area of decision neuroscience may be, I can't help but feel some discomfort at the coolness of the analysis, the desire to fit the behavior into a tidy box. As reliable as biology can be, I know that my own shopping habit was rooted in so much more than any scientist can begin to fathom. My brain chemicals may only tell part of the story.

◆ ◆ ◆

As 2002 came to a close, the only thing my brain told me was that I needed to do something fast. I was on a slow bleed of credit card payments, trying to spit out the minimum of $30 or $40 or $50 per cycle, sometimes falling behind. It was like a plate-juggling act. Inevitably, one or all would come crashing to the ground.

On a few occasions, I had paid my rent late. Now in addition to my exorbitant rent, there were monthly $100 late fees. Sometimes, I would find myself skulking in and out of the lobby like a criminal, trying to avoid Roberta, the building manager.

Of course, I was trying to keep this part of my life hidden.

I was especially careful to continue concealing things from my girlfriends. I didn't want any of them to know how dire things were becoming. It wasn't because they wouldn't understand; it was just that, by comparison, I looked like a terrific loser.

I had surrounded myself with a clutch of girlfriends who were hugely successful. One was a lawyer, one owned her own hedge fund, and another had her own fashion forecasting business. Deanna had put herself through five grueling years of school and had finally become a well-paid physical therapist.

The disparity between their lives and mine seemed to have come into sharper focus. I had managed to earn decent money over the years, but not nearly enough to afford the same lifestyle that some of my girlfriends now had.

My friend Leeta, for instance, had built a lucrative interior design business. She too loved clothes; she loved to shop and loved the most expensive and beautiful things. However, she was one of the few who could afford it.

She was thinking of buying her first home and was about to open her first retail shop. We couldn't have been on more opposite financial poles.

When she suggested that we take a trip to a yoga retreat in Mexico, I couldn't even begin to explain that it was something I couldn't afford. I wanted to believe I could afford it. And like many of my purchases, I rationalized the trip by telling myself it was "okay" because I needed a break.

With my American Express still in working order for a few more weeks, I booked my flight and my half of the down payment for the retreat.

Again, I told myself that I had checks coming in and that I would manage to get more work. This was another aspect of my addictive behavior, the constant denial, and the justification. Yes, I would get more work. It would come. If I wanted it badly enough, it would come.

♦ ♦ ♦

As Leeta and I barreled along the dirt road in our rented jeep, I felt a renewed sense of self. The sea was visible from the road, the sun was shining, and I was going to celebrate my birthday at a peaceful yoga retreat with one of my favorite girlfriends. The problems of the world seemed far away—if I just had time alone to think things through I could work out my situation and get back on track in no time. The only way I had been able to achieve this in the past was to let a man come into my life, but I was determined not to allow this again. I had just put the final seal on my relationship with Warren. I wasn't interested in a man pulling me out of the quicksand. But I remained naively hopeful that my desire to change was the critical ingredient in making the change. A steady diet of vegetarian food, yoga, and massages would help me.

While we walked along the beach, I explained to Leeta that I had effectively put an end to my relationship with Warren. She suggested I meet a friend of her ex-boyfriend, an artist named Udo. The last thing in the world I needed was a struggling artist. Again, I was in denial. I had dumped one of the wealthiest men in New York and was being seduced by the description of an artist who apparently lived in a messy loft.

In yoga class, I noticed a woman staring at me. She was tall and thin and had shoulder-length ginger-colored hair. After class while standing at the juice bar, she struck up a conversation. She was there with her daughter, who was celebrating her eighteenth birthday. They were doing mother-and-daughter things the entire week: mud baths, tarot readings, hanging out on the beach.

Leeta and I invited her for lunch, and that afternoon we learned her fascinating story. She was Irish, had married a member of Parliament, and had a child. Then there was a divorce, a retreat to France, and her new life as a contributing editor to women's magazines. In her youth, she had opened a boutique with a girlfriend in London and rode out the sixties in a haze of sex and drugs like many of the young girls of that era. She talked about how different things were for her own daughter, who was driven to school in a chauffeured car and had already seen half the world.

I found her wise and extraordinarily gentle in her manner: patient, interested (she asked questions and listened carefully), and she reminded me of my own mother. She appeared to be roughly the same age my mother had been when she died, and this made me realize that my mother would forever be frozen at that age. In the same moment, I realized that I had tried to freeze myself in time too.

There I was in Mexico; it was my birthday. I was no longer in my late twenties but had now reached my forties. Time was moving forward; I was getting older. Was I ever going to grow wiser?

These thoughts made me wistful and impatient with myself. I found myself struggling to hold back tears, and I wanted to go to bed.

That afternoon Leeta and I rambled down the unpaved road that led to a tiny village, which was no more than a short row of bars, restaurants, and shops. We found a boutique that stocked all kinds of unique accessories: quaint locally crafted things. I picked out a large chocolate-colored shawl, two handmade belts embellished with seashells and vibrant colored beads, and a necklace that I would later lose on the beach. I hoped that my American Express card would work.

It did.

Eleven

THE DIRTY
LITTLE SECRETS

I was continuing on my steady downward spiral.

There would be no easy way out, no overnight solution, and no instantaneous death followed by a Phoenix-like rebirth. I would continue my back and forth, my two steps forward, one step back. I was like an alcoholic who had trouble staying on the wagon—there would be days where I could go without even thinking about shopping, and then others where I'd fall from grace. The way an alcoholic might be found clutching the bottle, I'd be found clutching the Barneys bag.

I knew I had a problem, that was my first step to recovery, but I also knew that things might get worse before they got better. I would have to endure the process. I was trying to escape my addiction, but I would end up sublimating it with a new form of self-destruction.

It has been said that compulsive shoppers often display symptoms of other compulsive behavior. Very often, compulsive shoppers display signs of depression, may have eating disorders, or even exhibit bipolar tendencies. I had my bouts of mild depression but had never displayed anything more dramatic than that.

My obvious default, on many occasions in the past, had been men. I had frequently turned to men to avoid some of life's difficult moments. Indulging myself in a romantic relationship served as an escape hatch, and it provided me a way to feel without dealing with my grief. It could keep other demons at bay.

I had exhausted all other ways of avoiding myself and so turned, once again, to a relationship with a man.

I was attempting to become a woman who had control of her life, her finances, and her impulsive tendencies—but part of the process of removing myself from the shackles of all addictive behavior might mean delving into other bad behavior.

Meeting the artist, Udo, proved to be a necessary blessing and curse. A blessing—in that he provided an outlet for my addictive needs—and a curse in that he didn't provide any of the emotional or financial security and stability that I desperately needed.

From the moment Leeta started to speak about Udo, I was intrigued. I liked the sound of his name. I liked the fact that he was an artist, and according to Leeta, he was intelligent, sexy, and had just broken up with his girlfriend.

Two other things Leeta told me about Udo struck a chord in me: he wasn't rich, and he lived and worked in a messy rented loft in SoHo. I couldn't explain why, but something about his ability to exist in disarray seemed to be appealing as some kind of antidote to what I'd been used to.

I asked Leeta why she wished to set me up with such a man. "Perhaps," she suggested, "you'll have the power to reform him."

I was not interested in reforming Udo, but I did want to know more about a man who appeared to live on the edge. Maybe what I needed to shake my addiction was an artist like Udo, who wasn't concerned with the trappings of luxury, who devoted himself to creating meaningful art, and who could reacquaint me with a part of myself that didn't need to possess things to feel complete. At the very least, he sounded like a man who would be incapable of plying me with presents and so would be incapable of buying my affections.

I agreed to have Leeta contact Udo on my behalf. She concocted a story about my wanting to write an article about his art.

Two weeks later, I found myself standing in the doorway of Udo's loft, and rather than feeling like I had stumbled upon a bachelor's messy loft, I felt I had stepped into a fantasy factory. In many ways, the place was everything I hoped it would be, brimming with wacky creations and surprises. A young man who had his hair pulled back in a ponytail and wore wire-rimmed glasses greeted me at the door. The first thing I encountered was a large wooden worktable that held the entire dismantled skeleton of a horse. An assistant wearing a respirator mask was busy spray painting the mélange of bones in shiny silver.

The man who had greeted me noticed I was staring at the skeleton. He explained that it was a project for an upcoming exhibition in Zurich. "A beast on which you can get too close to the sun," he said, and I found this remark to be mysterious and intriguing.

The next thing I noticed was Udo, who seemed to glide into the room from the dark recesses of the long rectangular loft. He wore a light blue linen shirt—completely inappropriate for February—but it matched the color of his eyes and complemented his light tan. He was in his late forties, and his skin was etched with lines and furrows. I told him that he had the rugged handsomeness of a world-weary journalist, someone who had spent time in war zones and drought-plagued desert villages—too much sun, not enough hydration.

He had a captivating, booming voice, a Sunday preacher's voice, with which he explained that my assessment wasn't far off. He said that a portion of his career had been spent producing artwork with a journalistic theme and that he had traveled around the world doing art projects that drew attention to the plight of people who lived on the margins of society.

His most famous work was an ongoing project, a series of drawings, intricate flow charts, containing data relevant to social, economic, and environmental issues. He had created several hundred drawings, each decorated with graphics depicting things like world energy consumption, refugee migration, corporate power hubs, and predicted water shortages. He pointed out a wall blanketed in some of the graphically beautiful sketches.

It was only at this point that I stopped to look around. The loft was as Leeta described, a cavernous space overloaded with junk. My eyes darted around and lit upon a messy desk strewn with papers. Chipped paint from a radiator had settled like confetti on the floor, and a thick layer of dust coated the slats of teak window shades.

Being there under the pretense of wanting to write a story about his work, I had to act professional, so I pulled my recorder and notebook from my purse and started to ask questions.

I was attracted by the deep resonance of Udo's voice, which had the same reverberating undercurrent as the studio itself. The gilded horse skeleton, the mysterious drawings, and Udo all fascinated me. It was clear in my mind that I wanted to come back to this place.

By the end of the interview, Udo had asked me to have dinner with him the following week.

As someone who was forever searching for a way to avoid my true feelings, I immediately jumped into the deep end of the pool. I allowed the relationship to become the main focus of my life. If I tried to accurately describe what occurred over the next months, tried to put it in a neat, tidy box, I would fail. Udo and I did have a passionate relationship, but it was also a complex emotional relationship. At times, it felt like a battle of wills. At other times, it felt like a coconspiracy or even a form of therapy. We seemed to have agreed on an unspoken pact to accommodate each other's emotional crisis. I wanted Udo to help me in a last-ditch effort to avoid myself by becoming my new obsession, and I imagined he wanted to become my obsession to forestall dealing with his own creative angst. In the end, we failed on every level.

If anything could take me to the rock bottom that I unconsciously wanted to hit, it would be this. I allowed myself to become hooked on the uncertainties the relationship presented. Udo would sometimes disappear on trips and be unreachable for weeks. His relationship with his ex-girlfriend seemed to be unresolved. But this was exactly the kind of instability that I was attracted to at the time.

And I found that Udo played his role perfectly.

Still, during this time, my life appeared to be filled with bizarre and exciting possibilities. Suddenly, I found myself part of a team working on a film about freedom of speech and interviewing movie directors at the Tribeca Film Festival. In another quirky turn of events, I ended up on television, as a guest on the Comedy Network's *Tough Crowd* show starring the comedian Colin Quinn. I was asked to analyze reproductions of works of art confiscated from Saddam Hussein's palace at the onset of the Iraq war. The show was taped live, and my segment ended up being especially comical, although that wasn't my intention. In fact, I analyzed Saddam's works of art in earnest.

· The television appearance yielded a few hundred dollars and an unexpected offer from Quinn's agent to come to Los Angeles to pursue an acting career. As tempting as this might have been when I was twenty, at forty it held dubious appeal. I pictured myself arriving in Los Angeles with the best intentions but quickly going into a downward spiral if I didn't immediately get parts. I convinced myself that after years of weathering the hard knocks of a modeling career, it was absolutely ludicrous to pursue one that was even more tenuous.

But even if a move to Los Angeles had been the chance of a lifetime, I wouldn't have been able to recognize it. Looking back, I probably could have parlayed either of these performing opportunities into something lucrative, but I seemed to be more attracted to things that would bring me down. I was in a dead-end relationship, still shopping and living well beyond my means, and I was hell-bent on bringing things to a dramatic crescendo.

It was Anaïs Nin who wrote, "We do not see things as they are, but as we are." I seemed to be in self-destruct mode.

In the following months, my habit was to return home after spending a night at Udo's place and to immediately strip down and shower. I would start my workday with this ritual of cleansing and redressing. In many ways this was a lot like my shopping episodes; there was the me who had to make the purchase, was consumed by the desire to possess the object, and then there was the me who threw it in the back of the closet and never wanted to see it again.

Somewhere, in the deepest layers of my psyche, I had an understanding that the process I was going through was unavoidable, an exorcism of some kind, with the weight of years of grief and avoidance propelling it forward.

In lieu of being able to shop the way I used to, I had succeeded in turning Udo into my new addiction. As strange as it may sound, this attempt at replacing one addiction with another became a method of survival.

Survival.

That was the point. As much as my actions may have been self-destructive, the instinct to survive always kicked in. I had reached a point where I needed to borrow money in order to keep going. Although my work continued to pick up, I was now in a cycle of overlimit fees, late fees, and inflated interest rates on my credit cards. This contributed to a cash flow crisis.

One time I had to borrow $300 from my friend Kim in order to attend a press trip. I didn't have enough cash to get myself to the airport and back as well as pay for any incidental expenses along the way. Another time, I had to withdraw $500 from a trust my father had set up for me. Finally, I had to borrow several thousand dollars from a longtime friend.

Borrowing cash, it turns out, is an enemy of clear thought.

As soon as I asked for the loan (which he promptly declared not a loan, but a gift), I felt an immeasurable weight upon me. Of course, there was the release of knowing that, with the cash, I would be able to easily pay some overdue bills, but now the question appeared: what happens next? I couldn't go on borrowing indefinitely. I would have to face my finances sooner or later. If not, I could picture the scenario of me trying to hold on until I was evicted from my apartment. I ran the scene through my head: first, the electricity would be cut off, then the phone, and then perhaps I would stop eating. I would be found dead, and everyone would wonder what I was doing with all that stuff—new unworn shoes and clothing—piled up in the back of my closets.

But this was just a silly fantasy. The stories I knew about women who had to borrow cash were neither silly nor pretty. One story tells of a former model, who had racked up close to $70,000 of credit card debt. When her career hit a rough patch, she was unable to keep up with monthly payments. Things went further downhill when she became dependent on a boyfriend who was physically abusive. She eventually declared personal bankruptcy, but with no visible means of support, she was still unable to leave the abusive relationship.

Another story concerns a woman on the West Coast whose situation bore similarities to mine. She was a freelance-casting director with an unsteady income. She too had a penchant for clothing, felt the need to keep up appearances, and had borrowed money from a male friend. After she borrowed the money, the friendship became muddled, the conditions of the transaction unclear. I do not know the details of what happened, only that the friendship had suffered irreparable damage.

Borrowing money has a way of doing this: casting matters in a murky light. There were moments when I became paranoid about my own situation with my friend.

For example, there was a place he liked to frequent, a club in lower Manhattan. I had never wanted to go there. First, because half the men there would probably recognize me from the Hamptons, and second, because showing up at such clubs was tantamount to an inscribed announcement to all of New York society that you were a woman down on her luck. I didn't wish to encounter any familiar faces and was not prepared to officially declare myself an aging New York single woman who was reduced to perching herself on wealthy men's laps for a handout of a few hundred dollars.

But that's exactly what happened there. Between the hours of nine and eleven in the evening, it was master of the universe time. The top players from the world of finance gathered there, and of course, there would be women available to entertain them.

One time, in what I assumed was an attempt to stir my interest in this club, my friend invited me there for dinner. He had mentioned the place to me in casual conversation on several occasions, but that evening as we dined, I had no idea that we were in the restaurant that adjoined the mysterious club. As we stood in the foyer, about to leave, he asked me to follow him through the parting of a long velvet curtain the color of an aorta.

Suddenly, we were standing in a cavernous space filled with more heart-colored furnishings: overstuffed pink armchairs, divans covered in mauve chintz sitting in frames of ornate woodwork, and two chubby brown Chesterfield sofas facing each other like sumo wrestlers. Several round card tables were placed around the room, on top of which were satin lampshades festooned with thick-fringed tassels. The floor was covered in a plush carpet decorated with a complicated floral pattern. It seemed to absorb not only the sound, but also some of the limited oxygen in the windowless room. A huge multitiered crystal chandelier hung from the center of the ceiling. The place was crammed with all the froufrou trappings and gaudy extravagances unique to brothels and whorehouses for centuries, and I found it both funny and fascinating that such a place existed smack in the middle of downtown Manhattan.

I stood at the entrance and tried to picture what the room might look like when fully occupied, when all the fabulously successful men and all the needy women were gathered together and playing their respective roles. The small fringed table lamps would be illuminated, and plumes of smoke from fat cigars would rise like mysterious snakes in the air. Surely some ankles encased in strappy high heels would become caught in the jumble of carpet, and shimmering halter tops worn over tight skinny jeans would catch the prisms of light reflecting off the chandelier. There would be glossy white teeth bared, and heads thrown back in laughter, and curtains of hair that would fall over faces. And all of this would be a charade, the lacquer that glazes what was really going on there.

When I had just started modeling, barely in my twenties, there were girls I knew who worked as escorts in Japanese bars and dinner clubs in Manhattan. They had explained to me what easy money they earned just by sitting with Japanese businessmen, making conversation, and pouring sake. They always were offering to hook me up and get me a few nights' work at the dinner clubs if I wanted.

There were times during the years I was modeling when I needed to make extra cash, and working a few nights as an escort began to seem a rational and even desirable way to do so. A few times, I came close to offering my services, but I always backed out at the last moment. I found other ways to earn a dollar, mostly working as a coat-check girl, which wasn't nearly as lucrative and was definitely harder on my feet.

I always tried to picture what those Japanese bars were like and how those girls acted out men's fantasies in order to earn their dollars. As innocent as they made it sound, I am certain that there was more to the job than just pouring sake.

I remembered these moments as I stood at the entrance to the place. How was it that my life, almost two decades later, was offering up the same stale buffet? I was far too old to indulge offers of being a "good-time girl" of any kind, innocent or not so innocent. As difficult as my situation was, I could not imagine participating in any kind of seductive play in order to earn my keep. The idea of entertaining men for cash seemed far filthier to me than anything I would ever consider doing. And yet I found myself being in a vulnerable position, standing on the threshold of such a place.

My vulnerability left me imagining that my friend was indirectly suggesting this as an option.

Another time when another friend's generosity moved

him to buy me a gift, my paranoia got the better of me. One evening after attending a gallery opening downtown, I returned home to find a large black cardboard box smack in the middle of my studio apartment. I felt a momentary shock—did I enter the wrong apartment? Had the box always been there, and had I simply failed to notice it? Was I hallucinating? I walked around the box a few times, increasingly angry that someone had entered my apartment without my permission.

But then I read the side panel—Sony, twenty-seven-inch flat screen television. About a week earlier, I had revealed the fact that I didn't own a television. I had explained that I'd grown weary of wasting my life on shows that neither entertained nor informed me and that I'd rather spend my time reading and writing. I lied. The truth was that I couldn't afford to own a television. In my budget, there was no room to pay a monthly cable fee. I could barely manage my Internet bills each month. When I wanted to watch television, I went down the street to my friend Natalie's apartment, where we would make popcorn and watch episodes of *Sex in the City*, *The Bachelor*, and whatever new reality show popped up that week. I was always amazed by how easy it was to get caught up in these reality shows, which were no more realistic than a Grimm's fairy tale.

As much as I truly would have enjoyed owning a television again, it irked me that anyone would buy me such a gift. In fact, I should have been grateful that I had friends who saw right through my facade, my achingly convoluted attempt to appear in control.

I went to sleep that night feeling violated. It felt like someone had broken into a secret part of me and ravaged around in all those places I wished to keep hidden. Waking in the middle of the night, drenched in sweat, a swarm of questions ran through my head: How would I get my shopping and my personal finances in order? And what were my feelings about money? Was I afraid of money?

At one time, when I was graduating from high school, my biggest goal had been to earn my own money. I wasn't afraid of money back then. I grew up in a family that took money seriously. Nobody in my family had a problem with debt. I don't ever remember my parents owning a credit card. "Cash is king," my father always said. He carried a wad of cash wrapped in a thick rubber band. Living within your means was a simple concept: you spent only what you had or less.

While access to easy credit carried the promise of freedom and choice, the paradox was that it ended up being just the opposite. For most compulsive shoppers, access to easy credit sends them into a pattern of chronic debt. This appears to be true for a percentage of credit card holders in general. Statistics show that the average American pays approximately $1,000 in credit card interest rates and fees per year. In 2007 alone, lenders raked in over $18 billion in penalties and fees.

While owing money on a credit card was something that I could relate to in the abstract, borrowing the proverbial "cold, hard cash" forced me to confront my feelings about money directly. I realized that these feelings were deeply emotional. Money was tied in with love, security, and safety, perhaps even guilt. I thought back to my first big modeling paycheck that had left my father silent. Over the years, I had tried repeatedly to understand my feelings about that situation. For all I know, I could have completely misread my father's reaction. I've never bothered to ask. In all likelihood, he probably doesn't even remember the event. But for me, that story reverberated throughout my entire financial future. In all of my relationships, I have handed financial responsibility over to a man.

One of the unexpected side effects of borrowing money is that it jolted me into analyzing my feelings about the subject. Unconsciously, I understood that this would be an important element in my eventual recovery.

I kept the money in the top left drawer of the antique file cabinet that I had purchased at an antique furniture store on Bond Street. Its drawers contained everything important to me then: my magazine clippings, my journals, a Mont Blanc Agatha Christie pen set, and an eraser that my mother had bought me for Christmas when I was a child. The eraser, large as a candy bar and the color of a tongue, had the words *I never make big mistakes* printed in black Times Roman type across one side.

The cash was nestled in a cluster of pens, rubber bands, mini Post-it Notes, some loose change, and various postcards. I tried not to look at the cash, but instead would slip my hand in the drawer and fondle it. The wad had its own temperature and texture, and I liked to squeeze my fingers around its girth as if it were something that had a life of its own.

I knew what I needed to do with that money; I needed to pay bills. And I knew that if I managed to catch up on my credit card payments, I could start answering my phone again. The nagging calls of credit collectors, their barking voices, intimidating questions, kept me from feeling free in my own home. Each time the phone rang, I felt my throat catch.

Life could certainly start to return to normal if I took a few simple steps to get things back in order. It could be as easy as righting the steering wheel as the car began to swerve off the road. Small adjustments, that's all. I wouldn't have reached my destination, but I'd still be on the road. That, in itself, sounded like a return to normalcy.

A large chunk of the cash did go to pay two months of rent, but that still left enough to pay the minimum due on all of my plastic. If I had been able to find the discipline to do this, I would have also been able to eliminate exorbitant late fees. There must have been hundreds of dollars in monthly late fees at that point, but I wouldn't have known since I had stopped opening my credit card statements months earlier.

So I continued to hold out. Not only did I want to keep this stash of cash on hand, like squirreled-away nuts for emergency sustenance, I wanted to have it there to spend on something should I be overcome with the urge to shop. I wanted to know that I could go out and buy something if the wicked desire possessed me. I wanted to wake every morning with the security of this loaf of twenty-dollar bills that I could peel off and put in my pocket. I liked to imagine the money mysteriously regenerating itself in the darkness, cooking itself into larger sums, so that no matter how much I peeled off, a thick hunk would always remain.

Like a compulsive gambler I was living in that gauzy wonderland of hope — *my horse will come in* — and likewise, buying that Louis Vuitton handbag will make everyone want to hire me. All my financial woes will disappear, the right man will fall in love with me at first sight, and everything will be happily ever after from there.

My shopping habits had changed because they were forced to change. I was like a drinker who had to switch from champagne to cheap beer, or a heroin addict who could no longer get the pure fix and now dangerously toyed with a cut product. I was still out there, shopping, making my plea for the next high, and promising myself this would be my last. But the caliber of goods I could get my hands on had lowered dramatically.

While once I could step into the cool, marble-tiled corridor of Linda Dresner and be waited on by an attentive sales associate who knew me by name, now I was trawling the messy markdown table at Zara. Nobody called me by name there, not even when I handed over my credit card, which would be rejected. I would retrieve the useless wafer of plastic from the hand of the impatient cashier and then reluctantly pull my last twenty from my purse to complete the $19.99 transaction. The purchase would be tossed into a plastic bag, and I would exit as anonymously as I had entered.

But these insults didn't prevent me from shopping, nor did they prevent my persistent fantasizing about the transformative powers each of these purchases held. My embarrassment, if there really had been any, would quickly disappear when I hit the street. Then other emotions would take over. I would be overcome with feelings of disgust for not being able to control myself, and would worry about my financial situation. But I'd be swept up in a wonderful tornado of exhilaration as well. I still held in my arsenal of junkie beliefs the notion that whatever I bought had the power to change my life.

This must have been what I was thinking when I spotted the Balenciaga trousers stuffed between other "European designer" trousers on a rack at Century 21. Balenciaga, formerly a stuffy French couture label, had been injected with new young blood with the appointment of the designer Nicolas Ghesquière. I had been hankering for something Balenciaga for a long time, but at retail it was completely out of my reach. Balenciaga's prices were astronomical. Spotting the discreet black label and making out the B, the A, and the L felt like striking gold. I couldn't believe my luck! I had discovered these trousers and in my size.

They were ink black with a zip front and placard closure at the waist. The cut of the legs looked slender through the thigh and flared through the calf. I imagined the trousers could make my legs look three miles long.

And they did. When I stood in the fitting room on my

toes, the trousers hung in a straight line as if hemmed with weights. The extra fabric fell in a puddle around my foot. But my legs looked like they went on forever. The fabric was exquisite, a lightweight gabardine that wouldn't wrinkle

I slipped into my brown suede ankle boots and stood upright, turning in the mirror to check out the side view. In the heels, the length was perfect, falling just over the tip of the boot. Everything about them was absolute perfection, even the price. They only cost $171, a small fraction of their original retail tag of $945.

The ways in which I could rationalize this purchase were abundant. The fact that they looked so good was just the tip of the iceberg. Beneath that thought was the one about needing another pair of black trousers because the five or ten pairs already existing in my closet were all imperfect in various ways. Then the thoughts would run in quick succession like this: This pair will eclipse all the others and, yes, make everything wrong in my life start to go right. All the problems in my life stem from the fact that I didn't own the perfect pair of black trousers. What luck to stumble across them and at such a ridiculously low price. There is no way I can leave Century 21 without purchasing these trousers.

But at some point the rationalizing disappeared and my addiction, in its pure form, kicked in. The physical symptoms that often accompanied this part of my compulsive-buying episodes were now so familiar that when I felt them coming on I no longer panicked; I gave in and let them take over me. There was the heightened sensitivity to light, sound, and smells. The store seemed to become vibrant, bathed in a cinematic glow. There was the elevated heart rate, sweaty palms, dizziness, and general euphoric feeling. I felt I had been injected with helium and could rise to the ceiling if I wanted to.

Of course, I didn't have the money to buy the Balenciaga trousers.

Yes, there was still money left from the loan, but I had no idea how much was left or how much I had racked up on my American Express bill, the only charge card I still had and was able to use. I also had no idea if I had enough money in my checking account to pay my electricity and phone bills that month and if my rent would be late again. I was assuming the rent would be late if I didn't get a $2,000 check due from a client, which was likely to happen because checks from clients almost never arrived when promised.

Yet as I rode the rickety N train back uptown to my apartment, I knew that I would be back downtown later that same day, handing over my cash, clutching the ink black gabardine in my sweaty hands and imagining how fantastic I would look wearing my new acquisition...until I got them out of the store and wanted to chuck them in the nearest garbage bin.

In my sincere and efficient effort to self-destruct, I also started to neglect my basic nutritional needs. I had once known the benefits of good nutrition and was teased by friends for keeping a small stockpile of nutritional supplements in my refrigerator, but over the past few years, I had slowly let my guard down.

I kept a jar of change in a plastic Tupperware container on one of the kitchen shelves. Every few weeks I would go to the supermarket on Ninth Avenue, where there was a refrigerator-sized change machine that could ingest coins at an impressive rate and spit out crisp dollar bills (minus a small fee) in their place. It didn't take me long to realize that the Tupperware container never yielded much more than thirty-odd dollars and that was barely enough to buy food for a week, let alone fund any shopping I might have in mind.

My routine grocery list at the time consisted of a roast chicken, corn bread, a pint of half and half, a tin of Bustelo coffee, Total Greek yogurt and a large box of Grape-Nuts cereal. Occasionally I would buy something fresh and healthy like bananas or tomatoes, even some broccoli, but most of the time I found myself sticking with the familiar shopping list. I think it was because I knew just how much this list of items would cost and therefore would not endure any surprises at the checkout counter. I don't believe I relished a steady diet of Total yogurt and roast chicken, but I knew their price and knew how long they would last and how much money I had. That pretty much made the decision for me.

Food obviously was not my priority. And I still would rather have spent a few dollars on a magazine, a cheap pair of shoes at Daffy's, or even a pair of fishnet stockings.

My lack of concern for my health probably contributed to my overall feeling of malaise. There was hardly a day that

I felt good, and I was having trouble sleeping at night. I had started to notice bags under my eyes, and my skin was lacking in luminosity. It was clear that I needed to eat better, but I just couldn't be bothered to make the effort.

If I had to think of a word to describe myself during this time it would be *clenched*. Everything about me was pulled in tight and holding on. I was white knuckled and tight jawed. Once, when I was a young girl, I saw a neighbor hack into a golf ball with an ax to see what was in its core. At the center, there was an orb of tightly wound rubber bands. Now I felt like the center of that golf ball.

The way I dressed was indicative of this agitated state. Very often, I would wear a black leather jacket that buttoned up the front and was tight through the bodice, like a corset. I needed to be held together; the jacket would do the trick.

The jacket was from the label Loewe, and I had bought it for $1,100 on sale in East Hampton. For me, it was perfect, just a hint of fetishistic symbolism — black, shiny leather — and elegance. It had narrow lapels and two seams running down the front that looked like train tracks. The leather was smooth, but slightly too stiff and creaky, and this always made buttoning the top buttons difficult. This added to the armorlike quality and I can remember feeling contained, pulled in and bound, held together whenever I managed to successfully fasten all four buttons. Sometimes I would wear a fox fur scarf with this jacket, and that gave the whole outfit a slightly decadent feeling, although what I was going for was a softened look. The expression on my face was becoming hard, more angular, and I hoped the fur would soften my appearance. However, when I looked in the mirror, I couldn't help but think this bit of fluff only succeeded in making me look like a refugee from a Weimar-period nightclub. I wore the leather jacket with the fur collar throughout the winter.

I wore that jacket in the first days of spring, but when it started to get warmer, I began to take early morning walks in Central Park, and a pair of Adidas yoga pants and a gray cotton hoodie took its place. In fact, this getup began to replace not only the leather jacket, but also almost all other clothing. I would set out at 6 a.m. for my morning walk in those clothes and manage to wear them the entire day. I convinced myself that this was okay because they looked sporty, active, and comfortable. The yoga pants were probably five years old at that point and had grown several inches in length from the breakdown of elastic fibers. The hoodie fit snugly but was beginning to fade. I was proud of the way my body looked in this outfit because it showed off my long, thin legs, and when I walked briskly through the city wearing it, I felt like someone who was strong, someone who could rough up the city before it managed to rough me up. More armor. That's what it really was. More illusions of power or protection.

The hoodies and sweats were less about physical comfort and more about emotional comfort. It was easy to wear these items because they imposed no threat of judgment. Everyone in New York ran around town in some kind of workout attire, or day pajamas, as I liked to call them. Sometimes the more worn the garments, the more it seemed to indicate your commitment to a serious workout. My outfit, with all its shoddiness, was the perfect foil. It kept me from having to deal with a wardrobe that was looking increasingly out of style.

There were, of course, so many things in my closet that had never been worn and were now hopelessly out of date. The spoils of hundreds of shopping trips were settled like sunken treasure in the dark and dust-covered recesses like a seafloor of relics. Amid these relics were pairs of shoes, some still in their original boxes. There were shoes with soles that had never touched the pavement and shoes that had been worn only once. There was a pair of Calvin Klein riding boots, knee-high black leather with a $600 price tag still attached. There was a pair of Robert Clergerie black suede loafers with tassels and crepe soles that I had always hated because they looked so sensible. There were Jil Sander spectator pumps that I had bought in Hamburg, Germany, simply because they reminded me of a pair of beloved spectator pumps I used to own when I was in high school. When I was sixteen, I wore those shoes almost every day for a year and even refused to take them off for gym class. Also in the closet were five pairs of brightly colored leather espadrilles purchased in Mallorca at an outdoor market, all still in their boxes; a pair of Stephane Kélian wedgies woven from sea grass and nestled in a sea grass box; and one pair of Manolo Blahnik black velvet stilettos, which were worn on the occasion of my father's remarriage, where they got ruined by the rain.

Despite having this trove of shoes and boots to choose from, I went through that winter wearing one pair of brown suede ankle boots with three-inch stiletto heels, one of which was constantly threatening to break. The heel, in fact, had already broken once, and when I hobbled into the shoe repair for an emergency fix, I was warned that it would get me back home, but probably not much farther.

Instead of heeding this warning, I devised a plan. I would wear my beloved ankle boots but would carry a spare pair of shoes in my handbag. Throughout the winter I went everywhere with my brown mink tote bag, the one that Thomas's parents had bought for me at the Barneys outlet center in Long Island. It was a luxurious large square bag cut from sheared mink, a rich, dark chocolate brown. Inside, I stashed a pair of black leather T-straps with high heels and a square toe. These had been purchased at Daffy's on 57th Street and were from a cheap Italian label called Coco Pazzo.

One bone-chilling January morning, after leaving Udo's place, I stood at the bus stop on Sixth Avenue and Houston Street and could feel the heel trembling beneath the weight of my leg. Only a fraction of a second after this warning, the heel popped off and flew behind me so that it hit the glass of the bus shelter. I teetered and then was left lopsided, three inches shorter on one side.

As casually as possible and despite the subzero temperature, I proceeded to remove the spare shoes from my handbag, take the offending boots from my feet, slip my foot into the T-straps, buckle them, and retrieve the amputated heel just as the bus pulled up in front of me.

On the bus, I noticed two well-dressed women across the aisle staring at my lumpy gray wool socks poking out of the T-strap heels.

Was this as close to rock bottom as I was willing to go, or was it only going to get worse?

The crisis was in full tilt and showed no signs of stabilizing itself. I was peeling through my wad of twenties, and as much as my writing career was on the upswing, it was still not yielding enough income to put me in the black.

The credit hounds were growing more relentless in their pursuits. One terrifying phone call left me coughing up my last $500 as a settlement. A stupid move, executed in a panic, which propelled me into nonpayment status with all my remaining credit cards. This sent my credit rating into a downward spiral that would take the better part of a decade to recover from. I was flying without a compass and wishing I could just land somewhere, even for a short while, to get my bearings.

The only relief seemed to come from avoiding my life as much as possible. This had been my lifelong pattern, a pattern that I was evidently not yet ready to break. I began to spend less time at home and more time at Udo's cluttered apartment in SoHo. Tucked away in Udo's lair, I could forestall dealing with my own problems and quietly indulge my self-abasement.

I was comfortable in his chaos because I had no expectations there. By comparison, how demanding were the pristine white walls of my Southampton palace? How much was there to live up to? And how exhausted was I from that constant output of energy? How difficult was it to live up to the perfection that I had always been trying to emulate?

If my shopping truly was about a need to cope with my unresolved grief, my hiding in the foulness of a lover's messy apartment was a release from that need.

As a child, I would frequently make trips to the basement of our apartment building, where behind cagelike metal fencing, tenants stored their useless objects. It was a dimly lit, musty place piled high with empty corrugated cardboard boxes, discarded kitchen appliances, old tools, and various pieces of hardware. Amid this dusty maze, I felt I could lose myself. I could forget about the hard-boiled world outside.

Every once in a while, the building's janitor would hold a "cleanup" sale. Makeshift display tables—wooden planks on sawhorses—would be erected and items laid out. My grandmother would accompany me to this subterranean bazaar, and we would forage through the offerings, which were barely visible but for the thin ribbons of sunlight peaking through a few barred windows. I could spend hours there, if not days, rummaging through the junk.

On one occasion, I found a manila envelope filled with black-and-white photographs of locomotives. Until today, I cannot say what attracted me to this packet of images. I had no interest in machinery or transport or anything that the engines might connote. I can only imagine my latent interest in photography was what prompted my curiosity. I begged my grandmother to buy this artifact. The manila envelope and its contents — about twenty 8 × 10 high-gloss photos — went everywhere with me that summer.

Udo's stacks of old magazines and newspapers and tee-tering towers of books, dust-covered rows of DVDs, and the curtained-off room with colorful toys protruding from boxes held the same fascination as the junkyard wonderland, and perhaps the same hope of losing myself or discovering something to fall in love with.

As much as Udo's was a place of disorder, it was also a place of discovery. Just to look in the freezer could feel like an expedition. He often had exotic or unusual things hidden away: stingray wings from Japan, bags of miniature Hershey's Kisses, and rose- and lavender-flavored ice creams. The entire kitchen was a symphony of mismatched plates, utensils, and glasses piled around the sink in stacks and heaps. The white linoleum counter was decorated with circles of dried liquids. There were stacks of spices, tins of tea, tiny twin packets of aspirin, Italian licorice in their patriotic red and green boxes, Fisherman's Friend throat lozenges, herbal remedies, and overflow from small mesh baskets on the shelves of a baker's rack.

In the bathroom, there was more of the same: a rickety shelf crowded with a variety of shampoos and conditioners, several brown plastic bottles of hydrogen peroxide, half-used tubes of toothpaste, rusty razors, and numerous cans of shaving cream. There was a tub of Vaseline, greasy to the touch, and a tube of never opened Dirty Girl bath gel. A pile of soiled clothing was heaped atop a wicker hamper. The sink was caked with calcium deposits, and the faucet peppered with water drops.

Just outside the bathroom door, there was an old wooden table splintered in spots, above which was a metal dome lampshade punctuated with a single naked bulb. Late at night, I would sit at that table and listen to the hum of the refrigerator. Surrounded by the chaos, I felt cocooned in a safe calm. In those moments, I didn't ever want to leave that place and fantasized about ways I could keep myself there, silent and hidden. If I could have leaped into the file cabinet, I would have. But of course, this fantasy only existed because of its impossibility. I knew in my conscious self, the self that was still half buried, that it was just a matter of time before I would want to leave.

In physics, chaos is a temporary state between one natural state of harmony and its transformation into a higher form. The transition could be choppy. I was in the middle of transition.

Twelve

LOSS AND LOST

❧❦❧

When I wasn't busy aching with the desire to shop for myself, I was hoping for Udo to buy me things. And he did. Sometimes, it seemed like he demonstrated his own version of shopaholic behavior. On more than one occasion, he showed up at my doorstep toting a large plastic bag from Sears or Kmart. He had a proclivity for automotive things, hardware store tidbits, and curious food items. He also would buy himself clothing at discount stores like Daffy's and Century 21.

The first item he purchased for me was a synthetic padded brassiere from Kmart. It was the color of cheap face powder and the texture of a stale marshmallow. I hated it but pretended to be ecstatic that he had thought of me. He also bought me lingerie from Century 21: a peach-colored transparent silk camisole, a pair of coffee-colored suede lounge pants.

With the exception of the bra, Udo never allowed any of these items to leave his apartment. He kept them stored for me in a single drawer in a wall of black metal file cabinets: row two, third down from the top. Every time I left one of these items out on the bed, the sofa, or in the bathroom, I would return to find it had once again migrated to its filing place. The drawer was neither labeled nor in any way designated as mine, and this made me uneasy and suspicious.

By autumn of 2003, things were not changing for the better. We appeared to be reaching a point of no return. I was insecure, possessive, and constantly on edge. Udo had checked out. He no longer seemed interested in playing his part.

For Halloween we both dressed as vampires, the symbolism of which should have been freakishly apparent. I wore a Jean Paul Gaultier bustier-style vest that was so tight around the bodice I had to make sure I didn't breathe too deeply or laugh too hard. I paired this with a black ankle-length crepe skirt by the Belgian designer Ann Demeulemeester. The ensemble was topped off with a black velvet tricorner hat with a voluminous black veil that I had bought in Venice several years earlier. I coated my face in white powder and made two teeth punctures on my neck with lipstick.

Udo wore a black tuxedo and a black felt cape around his shoulders. He slicked back his hair, painted his face white, and had fake blood dripping out of one side of his mouth. We attended a party in a private room at an exclusive downtown club. It was a birthday party for Leeta, the friend who had introduced us.

I can't say I didn't feel envious of her. Leeta had managed to forge a successful interior design business on her own and was in the middle of buying her first house. Her life always appeared to move along at breakneck speed.

Leeta could afford to see a $1,200 Missoni dress in a shopwindow as she sped by in a cab and then call the store to order it without even asking the price. In contrast, I was simply stuck in limbo.

The photos from that Halloween evening spoke volumes. Udo looks like a down-and-out Nosferatu, and I look like a woman trying to keep up appearances. Even my Dior *blanc porcelaine* face powder couldn't hide the panicked look in my eyes. It also couldn't hide the strange skin rash that had started to crawl up the side of my jawline.

Two weeks after the Halloween bash, at a family gathering in New Jersey, my brother Stephan noticed the rash on my face. It had gotten worse and was spreading up toward my right ear.

"You really should go and see a doctor," he said.

"I can't afford one," I replied.

My brother took out his wallet and peeled off three hundred-dollar bills. He stuffed them into the pocket of my trousers. "Go and get it looked at," he insisted.

Just before Thanksgiving, I went to Century 21 and bought myself a new coat. Technically, I didn't use the $300 my brother had given me. I used what was left of the borrowed money. I had finally received a $2,000 check for an article about jewelry trends I had written three months earlier, and I put that toward my November rent. I was expecting another $2,000 very shortly and that would cover the December rent. January seemed to be light-years away, and so I decided that buying an inexpensive coat was the thing to do.

The coat I ended up buying was hideous; everything about it was wrong, but I bought it in a stupor. It wasn't one of my typical shopaholic moments where the store's lights seemed to brighten and the tunnel walls came up around me and all I could do was buy something, anything, to get me out of the place. It was more like a trance, as if I had been anesthetized. I had no recollection of trying it on, I only know that I ended up in my apartment with a tobacco-colored suede coat that was lined in a brown and white spotted cow pattern faux fur. But I took this as a sign that I was getting better. Maybe I had finally gone numb, and shopping was losing its appeal. Was numbness the first step on my road to recovery? If I no longer felt any of the buzz, the butterflies, and the euphoria that had accompanied nearly all of my purchases, maybe I had had a breakthrough.

I was determined to wear the coat, not throw it in the back of the closet, even though it was probably the ugliest coat I had ever bought. It may have even been the ugliest coat I had ever seen.

On Thanksgiving Day, Udo and I drove up to Woodstock to visit my friend Alexandra. She was still living on the horse farm after her husband had left and still inviting people to visit for holidays. It seemed we were all pretending nothing was wrong.

I was in the mood for pretending nothing was wrong, but the truth at that point was that just about everything was going badly. The only thing that showed any promise was my work, which somehow I had managed to not mess up. There must have been some part of my personality that refused to go down with the rest of me. I continued to garner new clients, more lucrative assignments, and turned out well-received columns.

I must have been a terrible sight. I wore the hideous cow coat that weekend. I tried to cover the rash on my jaw with some heavy makeup. It had stopped spreading but was moist and weepy. I had to continually dab at my skin with a tissue and reapply my makeup.

Udo's suggested remedy was copious amounts of hydrogen peroxide applied throughout the day and night until there was no infection left to bubble. I told him I was going to see a dermatologist after the holiday.

Alex's house was a carnival of barking dogs and sullen stable hands. Udo and I dropped our bags in one of the upstairs bedrooms and decided to go out for a walk in the backwoods before dinner. The landscape was stunning. The trees had lost their leaves and their spindly branches poked into the sky like reaching fingers. The ground was carpeted with colorful foliage, and the air was so crisp it almost hurt to breathe.

There were a few hours of daylight left. We set out across

the back lawn and followed the footpath that I had walked many times before with Alex over the years. But I had always been weary of traveling in the woods without someone who knew the lay of the land. I was a city girl through and through, and I was never shy about admitting my inability to tell north from south just by squinting into the sky. The woods, as much as I loved them, were more frightening than a crowded subway car stuck between stations. I asked Udo if he was confident he knew the way.

"Of course," he said, as he kicked some leaves into the air.

Three hours later, deep in the woods, we had no idea which way was home. The light was falling, I was cold, and I had begun to speculate how my ridiculous faux spotted cow coat looked in the middle of the woods. I was nervous but was desperately trying to act calm. It was apparent that Udo had no handle on the situation. "We're lost," he said, as if proclaiming that fact might somehow make him appear competent.

I looked up to the sky and hoped that some residual schoolgirl knowledge would surface, a sense of direction from the sun. No such luck. The sky was now covered with a blanket of clouds.

When I looked back at Udo, he was crouched close to the ground with his head between his hands, and it was here that some knowledge—for me, anyway—did kick in. Suddenly, it was undeniably clear to me that for almost my entire life I had been putting my trust in men to provide me with a sense of direction. Maybe it was nature—the clarity that fresh air, flora, and fauna can inspire—but in that moment, I felt I was having my first lucid thought in almost a year.

I wasn't sure how we were going to find our way back to Alex's house, but just knowing that I shouldn't rely upon Udo suddenly felt like a weight had been lifted. I squinted up into the sky but still couldn't tell the difference between north or south, east or west. No, my inadequacies hadn't remarkably disappeared, but rather than stand there paralyzed, I mustered up the courage to point toward a narrow footpath. "I think this is the way to go," I said.

Eventually we emerged on a lonesome stretch of road, and after about fifteen minutes of walking in silence, a small pickup truck came along. The woman driving said she knew Alex's farm and was happy to drive us there. There was no room for Udo in the front cabin; he had to sit in the flatbed in the rear. I remember looking back at him, watching the wind whipping through his hair, watching how he shivered in the cold air, and catching my own reflection in the sheet of glass that separated us.

If there is one thing that Thanksgiving marks, it's the beginning of the Christmas shopping season. And so suddenly, it seemed the whole world was on an extreme shopping high. The garlands of lights went up, the annoying Christmas songs were played over loudspeakers, and pedestrians carrying oversized bags of purchased goodies jockeyed for space on New York's festive sidewalks.

That year, for me, a minefield of questions accompanied the Christmas season. I was having trouble remembering what had compelled me to leave the lifestyle with Thomas. Why was I lingering in the relationship with Udo? And why was I risking greater financial peril by continuing to shop?

By the time Christmas Eve was near, my American Express card was unusable. I had $214 in my checking account and that had to last until the following week when a check was due to arrive. I knew my father, as was his habit, would probably give me cash to buy myself something for Christmas, and I was looking to that cash to carry me through the week.

And so at the last minute, I ended up buying Udo a small present, a paperweight in the shape of a building. For my nephews, I bought books. After that, I was flat broke. So for the rest of my family, I purchased magazines and promised annual subscriptions but never filled out the subscription cards. I can still remember giving my father and each of my brothers their copy of *Esquire* and promising the following issues would arrive. I even told myself that I would send the checks to pay for the subscriptions. I ended up only mailing checks for two of them.

I was embarrassed in front of my family that Christmas Day. They were kind enough to refrain from making any negative comments, but I could see that my brothers looked at me with concern and even some sadness. It wasn't that they were expecting a more extravagant gift from me; it was that they could see I was in trouble.

I wanted to shout out. I wanted to tell them that

something was wrong and that I needed their help. But I felt as if I were trapped behind a mask. I simply smiled, laughed, and pretended everything was fine.

There were other things that occurred at this time that served as catalysts for change. One of them had to do with death. It wasn't simply the death of my mother that I needed to resolve, but now the death of childhood illusions, the death of a former self-image, and the death of a beloved mentor.

I found myself on assignment for *American Photo* magazine reporting on the death of fashion photographer Francesco Scavullo. It was Scavullo, along with the fashion photographers Helmut Newton and Guy Bourdin, who had most influenced my early teenage self-image through their photographs on the pages of my mother's fashion magazines. I doubt I would have become a critic of fashion photography had it not been for the visual library I built reading *Vogue* and *Cosmopolitan* magazines since the age of twelve. Fashion images were my refuge, and in the flattened and compressed world of the magazine page, I escaped the imperfection of the real world around me.

Scavullo was credited with creating the Cosmo girl, the gorgeous hypersexual women who graced the cover of Helen Gurley Brown's *Cosmopolitan* magazine each month. I have vivid memories of standing before the mirror trying to emulate the pouty expressions of the Cosmo models, trying to push my breasts together to create cleavage.

Because my mother bought *Cosmopolitan* magazine each month without fail, I think I developed a particular fondness for Scavullo. I felt he was part of my childhood and part of my relationship with my mother. Coincidentally, he ended up in even closer proximity to my adulthood when he was a neighbor in Southampton. I would see him from time to time on Main Street or at the garden shop with his longtime collaborator Sean Byrnes.

In the late nineties, on the one occasion when I was asked to interview him, I showed up at his Midtown studio and felt such a familiarity with him that I walked through the door and blurted, "Hi, Francesco," as if we were old friends.

The truth was that I was nervous. Although I have interviewed some of the top fashion photographers of the last fifty years, I held Scavullo in awe. It wasn't that I thought he was the most talented photographer, it was simply that his images had taken their place in my psyche, and for this reason I felt a reverence for him.

I spent several hours speaking with Scavullo that afternoon. We sat in the lounge above his studio. Everything was white—a white couch, white shaggy carpet, and on all the white walls, there were fabulously large prints of Scavullo's disco era portraits: Halston, Liza Minnelli, and Sting. He spoke extensively about the model Gia Carangi, the one model I had idolized as a teenager, who died from AIDS contracted through her heroin addiction, and he told me about his sitting with Janis Joplin, which he described as one of his all-time favorites.

I remember that my hair was cut very short when I conducted that interview, and this was a detail about myself that made me unhappy. I must have harbored fantasies of Scavullo finding me a potential Cosmo girl. But for that my hair would have needed to be long, voluminous, and sensual.

So there I was in January of 2004 walking up Second Avenue on my way to interview Sean Byrnes. Scavullo was dead. This time, my hair was long, wavy, and thick. It was the kind of hair that Scavullo would have liked.

What strange twists and turns a life could take. Could that adolescent girl looking at the cover of *Cosmopolitan* magazine ever have imagined herself arriving at Scavullo's apartment in Manhattan on a cold winter day to report on his death?

And yet there I found myself, sitting on the sofa with Sean Byrnes in Scavullo's apartment. Sean was handling all of the requests for interviews and reports, but he seemed frail and shaken. I was surprised at how at ease I felt in proximity to his still very raw grief. But wasn't this exactly what I had done with my father after my mother's death? There were days, weeks, and months of sitting with my father on the couch, on the stairs, on the porch, on a rock in Central Park as spring was just arriving. Sitting and talking and listening to his stories and helping him get over his terrible loss. I felt there was a large part of me that had grown comfortable dealing with the grief of others and yet was still unwilling to cope with my own. That had become my style:

grief by proxy. So I sat there, as I had done with my father, and listened to Sean's account of his loss, his loneliness, and his grieving.

At one point in our conversation, Sean felt comfortable enough to read me a few of the condolence letters he had received, some of which sounded heartfelt and others hollow and insincere. Throughout, I was struck by my proximity to these intimacies—the strangeness of it all. I think I wanted to pinch myself a dozen times as Sean continued to read, his voice breaking in certain passages. How was it that I was sitting in Scavullo's apartment listening to Sean Byrnes read condolence letters from the socialites and celebrities I used to see on the pages of my mother's magazines?

As our meeting came to a close, Sean happened to mention that Scavullo had been on his way to photograph newscaster Anderson Cooper when the photographer collapsed and died. This seemed to trigger a spiral of thought: Cooper, strangely enough, is the son of Gloria Vanderbilt, whose family had owned the Moravian Cemetery in Staten Island where my mother had been buried.... Scavullo was born in Staten Island.... At eighteen, I bought a pair of Gloria Vanderbilt jeans.... I have a photograph of myself wearing those jeans, which were pale lavender corduroy.... My mother used to buy *Cosmopolitan* magazine at the grocery store, and when she returned from shopping, I would search for it at the bottom of the grocery bag, and there I would find Scavullo's photos.... Now, here I was writing a story about Scavullo's life and death.

This string of intertwining thoughts ran through my

head as Sean spoke, and I found myself tuning him out. My recorder was just about out of tape. I was happy the interview was ending and couldn't wait to leave.

As I rode down in the elevator, I realized I hadn't been to visit my mother's grave in over fifteen years.

Somehow, I ended up at Saks Fifth Avenue that afternoon. I didn't want to go home. I started walking downtown. I felt empty and afraid. That interview had thrown me off and now my brain felt like it was crammed with too many memories.

By the time I was standing in the middle of the chaotic main floor of Saks, I knew it was too late. I would never leave without buying something. I strolled past the cosmetic counters, and the scent of perfumes and lotions was intoxicating, almost too strong for me to stomach. The lights seemed to be extra bright, as if new bulbs had been installed in all the fixtures. The sounds—conversations, mobile phones ringing, high heels on the marble floor—all seemed magnified. I found myself sinking into this sensory circus as if it were as familiar as a warm bath. And it was. This was well-known territory. These enhanced sensations were all part of the fabulous undertow that I had grown used to over the years; it was the sensory magic that accompanied many of my shopping episodes. Apparently, my attempt at replacing one addiction with another was not working out, but I didn't care in that moment because I felt pacified by the familiar intoxication. The familiarity of my addiction actually felt like a balm in that moment. It felt like the most comfortable thing in the world.

I strolled over to a display case filled with sunglasses, and asked the sales associate if I could try on a pair of Chanel glasses with a titanium frame and iridescent lenses. They were spectacular. When I placed them on my face, they felt as light as a caress. The lenses created a colorful rainbow effect that reminded me of the rainbows made by soap bubbles. The glasses were $350. My American Express card was in my wallet. I had paid off the previous bill with some of the money my father had given me for my birthday. I knew I could use the card to buy the glasses, and so I did.

On January 23, 2004, fashion photographer Helmut Newton died when the car he was driving crashed into a concrete wall just outside the Chateau Marmont hotel in Los Angeles. He was eighty-three years old and like Scavullo had been on his way to photograph an assignment when he suffered a heart attack while behind the wheel of his automobile.

I read about the death on the front page of the *New York Times*.

I immediately thought I'd contact various editors to report on the death of this icon, but I didn't contact any of my editors that day. I proceeded to go through the motions of a productive workday, which, in fact, wasn't especially productive. Much of the afternoon was spent in my apartment, leafing through my oldest copies of *Vogue,* the ones that had originally belonged to my mother. I still had the one that first introduced me to Helmut Newton, the one from when I was fourteen years old. It was the one with the picture I had written about, a photograph of the model Lisa Taylor sitting with her legs provocatively spread while eyeing a man who stands facing her, his back to the camera.

The man in the photograph is a cipher; it is only a portion of his naked torso and long legs that we see and the shadow of his reflection on the wall behind her. The woman is the focal point of this photo, and she represents the new woman who was emerging in the early part of the seventies. In writing about this photo I have cited all these elements: the shadow of the man, the strong confident woman, the spread legs, the more than suggestive look in her eyes.

The caption beneath the photo says that the model is wearing a floral-patterned peasant dress from the designer Calvin Klein. It is available at Lord & Taylor and Bloomingdale's.

That day as I sat in my apartment surrounded by my trove of vintage magazines, I realized that I no longer wanted to be manipulated by fashion photographs. From the time I had been a teenager, I had managed to forge an identity based on appearances: clothing, accessories, and cosmetics. I had used the photographs presented in magazines as my road map. It was no coincidence that I had ended up writing about fashion photography. Unconsciously, I must have wanted to understand exactly what was going on in them. I must have always wanted to crack their code and comprehend why I felt they had so much power over me. It is impossible to deny the fact that fashion magazines and the photographs in them played a substantial role in my shopping habit.

"Fashion photography provokes viewers and consumers into confirming their own identity through structures of desire," writes Jennifer Craik in her book *The Face of Fashion*.

Those structures of desire are what continually left me hankering for more.

In recent years, women's fashion magazines have been targeted as the culprit behind many women's issues, mainly eating disorders and low self-esteem. Teenagers and young women are considered particularly vulnerable to these photos, since their self-image is still largely unformed.

I am not convinced that magazine images, just by virtue of their existence, can bear such blame. Rather, I believe, as some researchers on the subject have pointed out, an already unstable self-image may be vulnerable when viewing images that present an unrealistic ideal.

My feelings about this didn't come into sharper focus until several weeks after hearing of Newton's death, when I stumbled across a passage from a book about cultural images by Susan Bordo: "Today, teenagers no longer have the luxury of a distinction between what's required of a fashion model and what's required of them; the perfected images have become our dominant reality and have set standards for us all — standards that are increasingly unreal in their demands on us."

I was a teenager who had been insecure enough in my self-image and hadn't allowed myself the luxury of that distinction. When I read Bordo's use of the word *luxury* in particular, I felt a strong twinge of regret. That was a word my mother had often used and seemed to understand on a level that I had forgotten. She had spoken to me of "the luxury of tears" and the "luxury of being able to know oneself."

The fact that I had come to relate to luxury as something that could only be bought seemed especially tragic. I had tried to keep up appearances at great cost — both literally and metaphorically.

I would also come to realize that I could love fashion photographs, continue to enjoy them, but not be held captive by trying to emulate them.

There was one more death that served as a catalyst for change.

A few days after my birthday, Udo and I met at a Japanese restaurant in Tribeca where he informed me of the death of my former friend and mentor, Dr. Masao Miyamoto.

Udo knew that Dr. Miyamoto and I had kept up a friendship for several years, from the time I was nineteen years old to my midtwenties. He had heard me describe in detail how Dr. Miyamoto had taken me under his cultural tutelage and introduced me to everything from sushi to foreign films to exquisite French restaurants and contemporary art. Dr. Miyamoto had encouraged me to become a writer, had allowed me to accompany him to dinner parties hosted by United Nations dignitaries, and encouraged me to sit in on the classes he taught. His interest and belief in me functioned like an enormous propeller that pushed me out into a world that I might never have had the confidence to explore on my own.

Eventually, Dr. Miyamoto moved back to Japan, and we lost contact. I had heard bits of news about him over the years, and I knew that he had written a well-received but controversial book criticizing the restrictive nature of Japanese society. While I was living in Paris in 2001, I came across his book in the window of the Galignani bookstore on Rue de Rivoli. I can remember standing in front of the window feeling overwhelmed with a desire to see my friend and mentor again. I told myself that I would contact Dr. Miyamoto as soon as I had my life in order. I did not want to contact him when my life was in shambles and I was trying to figure out what to do and where to go next. As if he were a parent, I wanted him to be proud of me. I told myself that I would get in touch with him as soon as my life was more settled.

As Udo and I ate our sushi that evening, I began to recount the story of seeing Dr. Miyamoto's book in the shop window. As it turns out, due to his frequent trips to Japan, Udo knew even more about Dr. Miyamoto than I did. He told me about the fallout from the book (which turned out to be pretty big news in Japan's bureaucratic government circles) and how it had landed Dr. Miyamoto in a public relations mess that culminated in his losing his job.

At one point, I expressed a desire to see Dr. Miyamoto again and told Udo that I had thought of him often over the years and still held a singular fondness for him. It was then that Udo told me straightforward with no hesitation, perhaps more bluntly than I would have liked, that Dr. Miyamoto was dead.

I felt numb when I heard this, certain that Udo was

joking. "You're joking, right?" I said. Udo shook his head in that modest, controlled way of his.

. He went on to explain that he had read of Dr. Miyamoto's death on the Internet. He had died of cancer and was buried at Pere-Lachaise cemetery in Paris.

I started to cry, and Udo put his two hands on my shoulders and pressed me between them, as if he were trying to mold a brick of clay. I felt like a brick of clay.

Udo said he was sorry.

I didn't finish my dinner, and we went back to Udo's apartment. As I lay in his bed, my head swam with thoughts, memories, and emotions. I was stunned by the news of his death and regretted that I didn't try to contact my friend when I was in Paris in 2001. Then I realized it had already been too late in 2001. At that point, Dr. Miyamoto was already dead. He had died in 1999 at the age of fifty-one.

In that moment, I felt a crushing desire to see and speak to Dr. Miyamoto. I felt the urgent need to tell him about all my experiences over the years and what I had learned. I wanted to inform him that I now knew what it felt like to have a man take me shopping at Giorgio Armani, and it wasn't all that important.

It was the first time I had let such a clear, sharp thought on that subject enter my mind.

I was in no position to afford the lifestyle that I was trying to maintain. The bills were huge and piled on my desk, and most of them remained unopened. I was afraid to look. I was afraid of everything at that point. I was afraid to get out of bed in the morning. I was even afraid of Udo leaving me. But why? The thought of being alone sent me into a tailspin, almost a panic. I had become aware of my problem, conscious of my weakness, and because of that, I felt sad. I was sad because I still found myself unable to arrest the self-destructive behavior. I had acknowledged the problem. But my urges to shop hadn't miraculously disappeared.

One night, I made a list of everything I bought in that month: a pair of black leather boots, a black lace bra, a pair of Chanel sunglasses, six CDs, a cashmere V-neck sweater, countless magazines, and ten pairs of Wolford tights. All stupid meaningless things. The American Express bill was waiting on the desk with big numbers in the overdue column, and I felt myself swimming in a wave of panic. I imagined the card canceled for good, but maybe that's what I needed.

I would have to declare myself bankrupt. I would have to move in with my father, but more than anything else, I would have to stop, stop, stop buying things. I had to stop shopping!

How was it that I could remember almost every shopping episode I had ever had, but I couldn't remember the last conversation I had with my mother before she died? How could I remember the details on the tailoring of a Jean Paul Gaultier suit, but I couldn't recall what I said to Thomas when we parted? I couldn't express the joy I felt for my brother Stephan the moment I saw him with his newborn son, my nephew, but I could recall in vivid detail the giddy sensation of getting a package out the door of Century 21 and then inexplicably wanting to chuck it in the garbage.

If courage was needed to deal with my problems, I didn't feel I had any. In that moment, I only felt pain.

It was the shopping that caused me pain, and it was the shopping that gave me pleasure. It was both those things — the nourishment, the poison — combined.

Without shopping, I was afraid I would cease to exist. How would I renew myself? There, that's the dilemma: How would I renew myself? There would be nothing left inside me. Shopping had to keep coming to the rescue, filling up the hole.

I imagined that if Dr. Miyamoto were alive he would have been able to help me. If my mother were alive, she could have helped me. I couldn't keep calling on the dead for help.

I felt that my life would have to split open, so I could get a look at what I was really made of.

Thirteen

THAT CROCODILE DIED
A LONG TIME AGO

In the view from my apartment window, there were several things that fascinated me. Almost directly across from my window, a distance of only two avenues, I could see the white, windowless tower that my father had worked in for two decades. I can remember my father telling me stories about the building without windows when I was a child, and I had conjured in my mind a picture of him working in the absence of daylight, climbing the building's internal ring of stairs, emerging at the end of the day into the stinging sunlight. As much as I was fascinated by the fact that I lived in an apartment with a clear view of that very structure, it somehow made sense in my life.

The second thing visible from my apartment was a water tower perched atop a building several blocks farther uptown that would shine in the sunset like a gem, and it made me think of the word *Gotham*.

The third thing that I could see from my window was the swimming pool in the health club of the high-rise directly across the street. It wasn't that I actually saw the pool, but I saw the reflection of the pool in the health club's mirrored ceiling. And in that reflection, I could often see the body of a single swimmer doing laps in the otherwise empty pool. The swimmer was there almost every morning between 7 and 8 a.m. In my mind this solitary swimmer—viewed only as a reflection, a tiny body captured in light—was the embodiment of loneliness in a large city like New York.

As I prepared to make the call to the credit-counseling agency, I felt like the swimmer in the reflected pool. So much about me was small, removed from myself, afraid, and alone. I was completely frightened of facing myself and was afraid that if I did, I would find nothing there. I never saw the swimmer enter or exit the water; I only saw the figure pushing against the aqueous resistance.

As I picked up the phone, I felt a girdle of tightness around my chest and my breathing became shallow. My body seemed to go into an alarm state, a fight-or-flight state. In every heartbeat was an anvil's weight of dread that extended to my arms, which suddenly seemed to have gone limp. The telephone felt like dead weight. I wanted to put it down like I had so many times before, but this time I didn't. I held on, and I punched the number into the keypad.

When I heard the credit counselor's voice, I immediately felt relieved. He had a kind voice, not at all what I was used to from anyone even remotely associated with the word *credit*. He actually asked me how I was. "Not too great," I said with a nervous laugh. I had become accustomed to the aggressive demeanor of the retrieval agents, who tried to scare payments out of me.

I explained my situation: I estimated that I was carrying approximately $8,000 in credit card debt. This didn't include the balance on my American Express. He described my debt situation as "not terrible" and asked for the interest rates on all my credit cards, which I didn't have handy. "You'll have to get that information together and send it to me," he explained kindly. I'm sure I was not the first person who called without having these numbers handy.

The next step was to go over my income and living expenses to figure out an affordable monthly payment. As I began to calculate what my income had been in recent months, I could feel the blood rushing to my feet. To face the facts of numbers, the irrefutable bottom line, always left me panicked. The reality of what those numbers signified interrupted all my fantasies. I wanted to believe that I could afford everything I bought. In fact, I wanted to believe I could afford anything I wanted. In my imagination, there was no gap between what I was earning and the image I was trying to present—the fantasies I tried to maintain about what I wished my situation to be and what it actually was.

When the counselor heard the cold, real numbers, he was silent. He asked how I managed to live. How was I managing to live? I had been surviving by the skin of my teeth, by loans, by juggling payments. In retrospect, I realize that a sizable amount had been paid off in the previous year—all those "check by phone" payments made in moments of fear. Still, I had always fallen behind.

Things would not be simple, but he said he could help me. I would have to tally up my interest rates and give him the exact numbers on how much I owed. Again, the thought of doing this made my heart race and my chest tighten. The feeling reminded me of one time when I was scuba diving; my wet suit was too tight and the water pressure caused it to constrict my breathing. I started to panic underwater, thinking that I was experiencing some kind of dive-related illness, the bends. After a few seconds, I reached for the zipper and simply unzipped the uppermost part of my suit. The release was immediate.

Where was the zipper now? There was no need to panic.

My counselor explained that with applicable credit card debts (there were two cards which he wouldn't be able to help me with, for reasons I can now no longer recall) of approximately $6,800 and a rough idea of my income and monthly expenses, my payments would amount to $175 a month for a total of forty-four months. This sounded like an eternity. I would be spending years of my life continuing to pay for items that were probably nowhere in sight or stranded at the bottom of my closet, never used.

There are so many first mornings for addicts, so many "today it's going to be different mornings." I did not want that morning to be just another one of those mornings. I couldn't afford to go on wallowing or pretending that nothing was wrong and hiding behind other self-destructive behavior. Nobody was going to come and help me. I needed to stabilize the situation myself.

I don't know exactly where my resolve came from that day. It seemed to have sprouted up from nowhere in particular, and at the same time, I felt it had been taking root in me for ages. All of what I had been through in the previous months seemed to be pushing my resolve forward, like a flower that's been taking hold under the ground and finally bursts into the sunlight.

The relationship with Udo had finally ended, and despite my protestations as it sputtered to its inevitable end, I knew it was a positive thing. Maybe that was my last hurrah, my last stronghold against reform. Now having nowhere else to turn, my resolve to change had finally kicked in.

If I had been able to afford a therapist, I would have delighted in sitting for hours discussing all these issues: my destructive choices, my financial dependence on men, my compulsive shopping and subsequent financial woes, and my grief—I would have happily discussed them all at that point. I wanted to change; I could feel the desire to change had finally installed itself inside me. I felt I was finally ready not to avoid the difficult parts.

However, I couldn't afford a therapist and didn't know where to begin to look for a pro bono volunteer, and I still wasn't convinced that my woes would even be taken seriously. Despite the fact that I had started to read magazine articles about the seriousness of compulsive shopping, I still wasn't clear about the details. Would a therapist even take me seriously?

I allowed myself to be soothed by the kindness of the credit counselor and accepted that as the most talk therapy I was going to get, at least in that moment. And instead of just letting things go at that, I tried to invent my own therapy.

I did other things to make room for myself in my own life. I knew I no longer wanted to rely on an image of myself that was cobbled together from magazine pages and designer labels. What was I made of? What was my character? And what was my essence? The more I shopped, the less there actually seemed to be of me. To look in my closet was to see the costumes of a thousand and one people who didn't really exist. I wanted to see the woman who I really was finally coming into view.

Hanging on the wall of my apartment was a grainy black-and-white photograph of a lonely shadowy figure, beneath which, etched into the negative, was the word *nobody*. I had purchased that photograph from a friend, who told me that the reason I liked the image was that I felt like the figure in it. "You feel like a nobody," he had said to me without a hint of irony. I protested and bought the photograph in order to prove him wrong. It had been hanging on the walls of every apartment I'd lived in ever since.

I took the photograph down and replaced it with family snapshots. I made a pyramid of images that included pictures of my mother, father, and two brothers. I included the snapshot of me gazing at my mother dressed in her Russian princess costume. I included a picture of me on the beach wearing the dreadful eggplant-colored swimsuit that had been purchased with my father. I was tired of running away from these parts of myself and knew that I needed to be reminded of where I'd come from in order to know who I was, and what I could become.

Coming across one photograph in particular did propel me right back to where I'd come from. It was a photograph of me wearing my Gloria Vanderbilt jeans. In that photo I am eighteen years old, remarkably young and cherub faced and astonishingly blond. My hair is almost platinum and is pulled back in a tight ponytail. I am wearing a lacy V-neck sweater the color of grape juice and have matched it with my jeans — cords in the palest lavender. My boots are leather, the color of a breakfast biscuit with some cowboy stitching across the toe. They were my favorite boots at that time, and I can remember wearing them with those jeans as well as with a swirling circle-cut skirt in wool. That very outfit was worn one evening to Studio 54, and I paired it with a purple feather boa flung casually around my neck. I had no idea how young and blond I was, but I knew how good I felt wearing designer jeans and had no idea what that meant or what I was on the cusp of. It felt good. And when a paparazzo at the door of the club tried to photograph me as I walked past the velvet ropes, I placed my hand in front of my face to bar his lens, and my friends and I all laughed at this because I was just a girl from Staten Island.

Had I mistook that for meaning I was a nobody?

♦

Part of my agreement with the debt management program was to accept and read a book about personal finance and responsible credit card management titled *Credit When Credit Is Due*. One day I received the book in the mail, along with my scheduled payment contract. I can remember feeling my cheeks flush as I flipped through the book's pages. The language was childish, demeaning. It made me angry. It made me embarrassed.

Where was the smart girl I used to be?

I had once been a girl who worked a sixty-hour week in order to pay for her purchases in cash. I had once been a young woman who kept careful flowcharts of exactly how much money she earned and how much she owed on her newly acquired credit cards.

Now I was enrolled in a debt management program. I had also started to accept paid work from Thomas. I was writing copy for his product catalogs. As much as this felt like a humiliation, I had no choice but to buckle under the pressure to make money. The counselor had warned me that if I missed payments, I could be thrown out of the program.

Remarkably, during this time, a steady flow of new credit card offers continued to flood into my mailbox. There were zero percent interest starter rates, balance transfers, and rewards, all presented like enticing candy. Even with my lousy credit rating, I was still, unwittingly, a prime credit card customer. The chances were high that I would grasp at some of these offers and then fall again into the bottomless pit of late fees, overdraft fees, and inflated interest rates. Those offers represented cash that I desperately needed. It took Herculean strength to resist these offers.

But I did resist.

Then came the other phases to my rehabilitation process.

The first step, of course, was simply to stop shopping. No more Barneys, Bergdorf's, and Bloomingdale's. No more pilgrimages to Century 21, or pit stops at Zara. I can't recall with any certainty the last time I set foot in Linda Dresner, but there was a last time. It was years later before I could even bring myself to stand outside Dresner's windowed facade, and when I did, it was only for a moment, only to catch a glimpse of my reflection in the glass.

If there was one thing that stopping shopping revealed, it was the vast amount of time the activity had occupied in my life. How many hours had been spent shopping or having thoughts of shopping?

Today, when I read the results of surveys outlining the habits of compulsive shoppers, I recognize my former self. According to one study conducted by a United Kingdom–based debt management firm, of 280 people polled, 37 percent classified shopping as a hobby; 54 percent believed shopping made them happy; 33 percent excited. Another online survey conducted by U.K. *Cosmopolitan* magazine found that of 778 women, ages nineteen to forty-five, 74 percent said that they think about shopping every minute.

I am aware of shoppers who claim to spend eight or ten hours a day shopping. I was not one of those shoppers. Still,

I could linger in shops for two, sometimes three hours a day. For the past two decades, I had probably been in a shop almost every day of my life.

I can remember, in the year or two after my mother's death, I often went to Saint Patrick's Cathedral on Fifth Avenue to light a candle. After lighting the candle, I'd sit in a pew, trying to pray or simply collect my thoughts. These moments were never very successful. It wouldn't be more than ten minutes before I would become fidgety and have to leave. Because Saks Fifth Avenue was right next door to Saint Patrick's, I would find myself, almost mechanically, crossing the street and heading through the gilded doors of Saks. There, almost miraculously, my fidgeting would subside, and I would spend hours strolling listlessly, mindlessly, through the store.

To occupy some of the time that I had formerly spent shopping, I went for more long walks in Central Park. "Nature," wrote Thoreau, "which, if we unconsciously yield to it, will direct us right." Walking in the park was my attempt to be pointed in the right direction.

It wasn't just that nature helped me but also the fact that I could spend hours there for free, not needing to spend a cent, and be completely alone with my thoughts.

Many of those thoughts were anxious ones. My over-arching concern was for my future well-being, my financial future. Would I be able to continue to get enough work to pay my rent and pay off my debt?

How I had managed to avoid having conscious thoughts on this subject before seemed remarkable. Had I been so willfully out of touch with the seriousness of my problem? Yes, I had.

Still, the desire to shop persisted. My desire to cocoon myself in the safety of new purchases, which always held promise of new opportunities, hadn't simply disappeared. I knew I would have to tackle the myriad emotional reasons for my compulsive shopping, but I was still figuring out how to confront that. I can remember feeling great discomfort even thinking about a life without shopping.

There were moments when the desire took over.

One day, I found myself downtown on Canal Street on my way to buy a Tod's handbag. I had tumbled into the hole again. I had become obsessed with one style in particular, the same one that Natalie had bought for her assistant, a "bonus bag," for the good job she had done on a recently completed project. At Tod's on Madison Avenue, the bag sold for close to a thousand dollars. On Canal Street, I could get the knockoff for around thirty bucks.

I knew when I headed downtown that day that this was another impulsive move. If I had been rational, I would have spurned the idea of buying any handbag at all. I would have thought of my resolve and my financial situation. I would have thought of all the handbags that already hung in my closet. Moreover, throughout the entire "it" bag phenomenon of the late nineties, I had managed to stay clear of buying obvious labels, logo-laden styles, and the bag of the moment, opting instead for styles that were less recognizable and therefore would have more longevity. The Tod's bag was an "it" bag of the moment, and there I was hankering for a poorly made fake.

As I walked along the crowded street I was accosted by catcalls, "Prada," "Gucci," "Coach," "Vuitton." The stalls were fully loaded with handbags, wallets, totes, duffels, scarves and belts, all knockoffs of the latest styles. There were the LV's, the connecting C's, the big G, and proud H all on display. It was an entire alphabet of a burning universal luxury-world desire: to belong. There it was, the real and the fake, collapsed before my eyes. The items were devoid of any of the substance that had made them unique—the artisanship, the history, the exclusivity. They had been reduced to symbols. Nothing more.

I ponied up to one of the stalls and handed over my thirty bucks. It wasn't a lot of money; it wasn't going to break me. Yet as I did this, I got the sense that I was doing something also symbolic, perhaps a last symbolic act in a theater of my own manufacture, in a play that I wanted to finally see come to its rightful end.

The bag wasn't even beautiful. It was the color of a football, and it had a vaguely crescent shape. The familiar driving shoe nubs that Tod's was known for were sprinkled across the bottom of the bag, and there was a small pocket, perhaps for a mobile phone, on one end.

The bag was thrown into a plastic sack, and I carried it home. I put it in the closet, and never, ever let it come in contact with my skin again.

That symbolic purchase became a demarcation, a clear line for what I considered the end of my years of compulsive shopping.

I had used shopping to avoid myself. I had used shopping to define myself.

The challenge wasn't simply to stop shopping but to recontextualize myself as someone who was neither defined by her ability to shop nor her possessions. Unexpectedly, while trying to forge a new image of myself, I began to fear I would forget my mother.

While other friends lamented about how much they had begun to resemble their moms or how they reeled against her overarching influence in all their lives, I suddenly began to have the opposite emotion. I longed to see my mother again, even if just for a moment.

I started to seek other memories of my mother rather than simply avoiding them. This became part of my recovery process. Still no Phoenix-like rebirth in sight, but I knew I was making moves in the right direction. Confronting my debt via the credit-counseling agency (it felt good to be able to answer my phone again), recognizing my infantile attitude toward my financial situation, and coming out from under the cover of a destructive relationship were all positive steps. Yet part of my problem had to do with my unresolved grief. Seeking my mother, rather than trying to run from the pain of her absence, became one of my goals.

So I sought her in the photographs I possessed, in the memories I had of her, and in the few possessions of hers that I had inherited. I tried to remember the aphorisms she was most fond of using: laugh in the face of adversity and something about having faith. And then, of course, her observations about luxury. "I can't afford the luxury of tears," she used to say. Once I had asked her what she meant. She explained that if you have the time to cry, things couldn't be all that bad. "If they were all that bad, you'd be too busy doing something about it," she had said.

I also began to look through books that had belonged to her and the books she had given me when I was a child. There was *The Golden Treasury of Poetry,* a gift to me for my tenth birthday, in which she had written my name as owner of the hefty tome in the upper right-hand corner of the first page. There were two books from authors with the same name, Lee: her copy of *To Kill a Mockingbird,* which my brother had managed to deface with his childlike artwork, with the long muzzle of a hunter's shotgun aimed at a bird in the sky. Then there was her copy of *The G-String Murders,* the murder mystery written by the burlesque queen Gypsy Rose Lee. These books, with the name coincidence yet distinct personalities, reminded me of my mother's diverse reading habits.

There were other books too, different books, that made me remember different aspects of her personality. There was her copy of *Gayelord Hauser's Treasury of Secrets,* a squat, fat book that she had covered with an embroidered burlap cover. The book was a real relic, filled with out-of-date beauty advice. But that book made me remember certain images of my mother I thought I'd forgotten—in the kitchen, steaming her face over a cauldron of herbs; wrapping her head in a towel after applying a mayonnaise conditioning treatment.

And then, of course, there were her old magazines, the fashion magazines that I had managed to save and lug with me from apartment to apartment, from marriage to divorce, to the Hamptons and back into Manhattan again. Those very magazines contained all the photographs created by all the photographers — Scavullo and Newton among them — who had managed to leave such an indelible impression on me.

Finally, there were the pieces of clothing and jewelry that had belonged to my mother, all the stuff that was mingled with mine in the closet. I hadn't bothered to separate these pieces out, to designate them to a particular place. Instead, I had them scattered among my own towers of turtlenecks and T-shirts or in the sloppy stacks of rarely worn trousers, sweatpants, and skimpy summer tops. In total, there were only four items of clothing of hers I had kept: a black-and-white bull's-eye patterned sweater with big plastic buttons (very Mary Tyler Moore), a purple halter top, her Betsey Johnson moon-and-stars blouse, and her black satin palazzo pants.

In the only notebook I have of my mother's, one that contains her thoughts and words, she had written: "I made up my mind to change, and I did so with a vengeance."

When I read these words, several years after her death, I was startled. I had no idea what she was referring to. Did this have something to do with her mystery, that distant part of her that I was forever trying to reach? In some ways, the sentence made perfect sense: my mother was a glutton for self-improvement regimens even before they became an American phenomenon. But what was it about herself that she was so intent on changing?

I decided to take this as my motto and try to live up to my mother's words.

Other challenges awaited me.

When a French film director who had been pursuing me for almost a year showed up at a party one evening, I was surprised to find that I felt happy to see him. It was at a party at the Maurice Villency furniture store on Madison Avenue.

In a corridor of the crowded party, I stood watching the scene take shape. The place was packed and buzzing with excitement. And like Andy Warhol, I found myself saying hello to lots of people who said hello to me. But that night, I felt worn out from the exercise. I was tired of speaking to people who didn't really care about me or what I had to say. Yet there I was, nourishing my undernourished self on miniburgers and salmon tarts and glasses of free champagne. I had become one of those peculiar New York women who frequented such parties simply in order to eat.

Or maybe the problem was that I was no longer the neophyte. There had been a time when these parties seemed exciting, even exhilarating. Now, looking around the room I could see that none of it had any meaning.

The crowd undulated in its usual way, ebbing and flowing with the trays of food and drink, the temperature, or the appearance of a minor celebrity. Here we were, once again, at a furniture showroom and celebrating exactly what? I had no idea. Did every new furniture collection need to be celebrated?

I spotted the French film director across the room and felt a faint wave of delight. This was completely unfounded: I hardly knew the man and had actively avoided his advances for almost twelve months, but now I was suddenly ready to give him the time of day because I was lonely.

The date with the Frenchman was on a Tuesday night. We were to have dinner at Jean Georges, which seemed to be where many of the recent episodes of my life were destined to play out. I had one outfit that I wore often during that time because it felt safe. What I mean by safe is that I could get away with wearing it and not feel that it looked too dated, out of style, or shabby. It was a red silk skirt that had been purchased in a seaside resort town of France called La Rochelle back in 2001. I paired it with a red and blue checked stretch polo shirt. When I had gone to interview Paris Hilton for a magazine story, she had noticed that shirt and complimented me on it. I took that as a badge of hipness, a passing grade. The shirt would pass muster.

When I arrived at the restaurant, the Frenchman was already there, having a drink at the bar. He got up to greet me, kissed me hello, and suggested we sit at our table right away.

As soon as we were seated, I began to get a whiff of his disagreeable personality. He complained about the presentation of a plate of bread and olive oil; he commanded the waiter like a drill sergeant. Was he trying to impress me? Some men think bravado is an aphrodisiac. I watched as he fidgeted with his appetizer, some *mille-feuille* of vegetables. "It's not right," he protested and threatened to send it back. The wine, he said, was "not the correct temperature."

By the time dessert arrived, things had sufficiently calmed down and we were able to share a few laughs and get to know each other. He talked about his difficult childhood, his absent father, how he missed France, and how happy he was that I had finally accepted his invitation to dinner. Naively, I took the bait and melted into a litany of my own revelations. I was lonely and afraid at that point in my life, and I could feel that my desire for closeness with a man, once again, was outweighing my sense of self-protection. My first instinct had been that I didn't like this man very much and that explained why I had put off his advances for nearly a year. Yet there I found myself, in desperation, decanting my soul.

I had my hands clasped on the table as I spoke. At some point, the Frenchman reached over and grabbed them. He held my left hand in his, and then he started caressing the inside of my arm. It felt soothing and encouraged me to keep speaking. A moment later, I realized the caressing had stopped. The Frenchman was examining the wrist on which I wore the Jaeger-LeCoultre watch. That watch had been the last Christmas present from Thomas.

I explained that it was a Reverso watch, the kind that had been originally designed for polo players to wear and that the band was crocodile.

The Frenchman lifted my arm slightly in the air and held it closer to his face. I thought he was going to kiss my arm or my hand or do something equally flirtatious and French. Instead, he said, "That crocodile died a long time ago," and he placed my arm back down on the table.

I pulled my arms away and held my right hand over the offending watch. I could now see that beneath the restaurant's overhead lamp, the band did look old, cracked, and faded. It was true; that crocodile had died a long time ago.

"Yes, it did," I agreed, forcing myself to giggle about this fact. The Frenchman smiled weakly.

He proceeded to summon the waiter and paid the check and we stepped outside into the buzz of Columbus Circle. I was happy to have all the street noise as a distraction and the relative darkness of night to hide anything else he might find wrong with me. He came up behind me and hugged me tight, nuzzling his chin into the back of my neck. We started to walk toward my apartment, and passing Duane Reade, I insisted that I had to quickly go in and pick up a few things. "I'll wait outside," he said.

I stood in line with my toilet paper, toothpaste, and coffee. I wasn't sure if he wanted to come up to my apartment or not. I needed to buy these things just in case. Out of necessities — that seemed to be the story of my life. But as I stood beneath the glare of the store's hard fluorescent lighting and the effects of too much wine began to wear off, the sting of his insult started to rise inside me like a welt. I asked myself why I was still willing to accept this kind of brutality from men. And if I did, how was I going to stay on a positive track?

I stepped out of the store and onto Eighth Avenue and discovered the Frenchman had gone.

♦

I once heard that sales associates in luxury shops size up a customer's buying power by looking at his or her shoes and watch. Supposedly, these two items most reliably indicate wealth. If the shoes and the watch carried enough status, the sales associate would kindly offer service. If not, the customer would receive nothing but a cold stare.

I knew about the overzealous attentions of sales associates, and I knew about cold stares. I hadn't realized that my watch would no longer make the grade. Time ironically had taken its toll on my once prestigious wrist piece.

Trying to keep up appearances had reached its conclusion. It had sputtered out with this sad and revealing restaurant scene. And as much as I wanted to cling to the juvenile thought processes that had me on the phone with my friends describing myself as a "victim" of the disappearing Frenchman, I knew I was not. I was only a victim of myself. This, it turns out, is a fact much harder to swallow. Because when I began to tally things up, it came out to this:

As I had hitched myself to marriage and pinned my financial well-being to his, I had equally managed to badly navigate my next serious relationship. And as much as Thomas had truly loved and cared for me and kept me cocooned in his protective force field, I became the classic bird in a gilded cage, the kind who stops singing and withers away, forgets how to fly. I didn't want this to continue in the same trajectory, but at midlife, it is more than difficult to take a different tack. And yet what was clear was that I had run out of options. I did not want to be owned, bought, or consumed. I wanted a relationship that was based on love and respect and not couched in neediness, substitute mothering, or sexual or financial dominance.

I had gone through my entire adult life trying various lives and shopping styles on for size. Part of my desire to shop may have been rooted in my desire to keep myself as the product. How else did I know how to relate to myself? No longer consuming, just being consumed, was the way I looked at it.

If I stopped to examine my credit card statements, I would have realized the consumption was extending far beyond what I even knew. My interest rates on some cards had been an astronomical 36 percent, and I was too afraid to make a phone call to even question why.

It wasn't very different from the behavior of other addicts who are usually very savvy and manage to fool everyone around them, who are aware of the choice between right and wrong, but who get some sinister pleasure out of circling back to the very thing that they should stay away from and pouncing on it, sinking into it, succumbing to it, and then later regretting it.

I had reached the point where all this would end.

Fourteen

AFTER THE FALL

———— ❧ ————

S hopping for emotional and psychological reasons has become the new mantra of modern society, says Jim Pooler in his book *Why We Shop*. According to Pooler, modern shopping revolves around self-actualization. Living in an affluent society, where all basic needs are met, leaves space for this kind of emotional shopping.

In *The Soul of the New Consumer,* authors David Lewis and Darren Bridger echo Pooler's observations and describe affluence as freeing up New Consumers to devote "more time, effort, and energy to closing the gap between their real and ideal selves." Surprisingly, they also acknowledge the inherent risk: "Unfortunately, the harder we strive to attain our ideal self the further away it seems to be, and the wider the gulf that exists between it and our real self."

It is the shopping addict who knows this best.

It was this kind of emotional shopping—the mindless

242

acquisition that I had become accustomed to. By the time I made the decision to stop, both my emotional and basic needs were hardly being met. My health—both physical and financial—was suffering, and the self I had wanted to actualize barely existed.

A closet so full...so empty inside.

In 2004, there were still too many jokes about shopaholics and limited discourse on the serious consequences of overspending. Chick-lit novels, whose characters spent their way into richer, more fulfilled lives, and the women of *Sex in the City* presented anodyne versions of the modern, urban female shopper. I knew what it felt like when "moi" from *Bergdorf Blondes* discloses her love of sample sales and Chloe jeans. And I knew what Carrie Bradshaw was talking about when she realized that she could have put a down payment on an apartment with the dollar amount represented by her collection of shoes.

But I now also knew something else.

There did come a point where I wanted to understand how I might, one day, begin to shop again in a way that gave me pleasure, fulfilled my needs, without interfering with my life. I believe I wanted to regain the ability to purchase things as an addition to myself, not as a way to avoid myself.

There were stages in this pursuit that perplexed and frustrated me.

There was a short period where I became fearful of making any purchases at all. I was afraid of making a mistake. There were months where, even when I absolutely needed something, I found myself terrified of going through the act of buying it. On one occasion, when I needed to buy a new pair of sneakers because my old Nikes actually had a hole worn through the toe, I found myself standing before a wall display, with tons of styles to choose from, drenched in a sweat of anxiety.

I left the shop without buying a thing.

Eventually, this anxiety went away. I was able to achieve a balance and feel confident about my purchases. I began to trust myself with money, responsibility, and the knowledge that I now knew the difference between wants and needs and how to allow myself both at the appropriate times.

When I did start shopping again, I realized that my feelings about shopping had changed. I was no longer plagued by an itch that said, *buy something, you must.* There were no more butterflies in my stomach. This change gave way to other thoughts, and one of the things that occupied me was instant gratification. So many of my shopping episodes were marked by the impulse to buy, the "must have" moment. The credit card came out; the purchase was packed. Almost always, there was a way to get instant relief for my urges.

I thought back to my eleven-year-old self and the beloved baby blue wedgies. I had to wait a full year to wear those shoes, and when I did finally wear them, it was with an almost unbearable pleasure.

On my road to recovery, there were other concepts that

occupied my thoughts. I thought about mindful acquisition as opposed to mindless acquisition. The idea wasn't to reject shopping completely, but to understand how I could make meaningful choices in my shopping. To understand, in fact, how I could shop consciously.

I began to think about the concept of enough: When would I have enough? When would I be enough? So much of my shopping had stemmed from feelings of inadequacy, inferiority, and low self-esteem. Enough on the outside could never be achieved if I didn't feel I was enough on the inside.

◆ ◆ ◆

Change.

Change with a vengeance.

In the Merriam-Webster dictionary the many definitions for change include "to give a different position, course, or direction; to become different, to undergo transformation, transition, or substitution; to put on different clothes."

If I looked in the closet, what would I see? How was the changed me going to cope with everything that existed there?

When I finally decided to clean out the closet, it was not because I had given up on all the people I used to be who were still suspended there. It was because I was finally moving to a new apartment.

In emptying my closets, I was forced to confront all the women I used to be or thought I was or wanted to be over the years. I had to confront some of the unopened bags that still took up residence on the floor, and question myself as to their meaning, their value, and why those items had once seemed so important to me. I had thought of my clothing as my autobiography.

In sorting things, there were decisions about what would be kept and what would be discarded. I also realized that I had never been able to sell any of these items because I related to all of them as being parts of me. The thought of a stranger wearing any of my items of clothing was untenable.

Oddly, for reasons I cannot explain, I did not apply this rule to shoes. I ended up giving many pairs of shoes to my friend Kim, with whom I shared the same shoe size.

As for the other items, some, of course, were easier to part with because they were damaged or eaten away by moths or no longer fit. The Gaultier suit, the one that had dramatically demarcated a turning point in my life, was still there. The fabric of the pants was worn, threadbare in spots. The armpits were torn as well.

To see it was to be reminded of the change instigated by its purchase, the way it interrogated the other lesser items in the closet of my tiny studio apartment where it first hung.

To see it was to be reminded of the French essayist Diderot, who in the eighteenth century wrote about the perils of being dissatisfied with one's possessions based on the arrival of a new, superior item. In his case, it was the arrival of a new dressing gown that set off a spiraling dissatisfaction, leading him to replace almost all his worldly possessions with newer, better versions. In the end, Diderot reflects on the resulting disharmony, stating, sadly, that there was "no more consistency, no more unity, no more beauty."

Was my closet a modern version of Diderot's? My Gaultier suit, the equivalent of his famous dressing gown?

There were other items in my closet, which didn't look like they could have ever belonged to me. They looked like something another woman might wear. Some were cut so strictly and severely as to look monastic. They were all in shades of gray.

Other things were easier to part with: unworn underwear, the fake Tod's handbag, the stiff, blue tulle skirt that refused to yield to doorways.

However, when I came across a black velvet skirt — a skirt that had been purchased on one of my earliest trips to Paris — I felt a great surge of empathy for the young woman who wore that skirt. That was a young woman who had fallen in love and then was disappointed in love, a woman who had no idea of the twists and turns her life would take.

That skirt had stayed in my wardrobe, and it would stay. It would continue its silent life there.

What I also thought would stay was my anorak. It was army green with a gold satin lining and fur trim around the hood. There was a drawstring at the waist, and it was reversible. I only wore it on the green side; the gold was too loud, ostentatious. It didn't suit me. But sometimes I would wear it unzipped and it would flap open in the wind, and then the gold would peek out like bursts of sunshine coming through clouds.

That anorak had once been in a fantastic dream. In the dream, I had thrown it away, but it had mysteriously showed up again in my closet. When I discovered it there, I was happy to see it, as if it were a lost friend who had suddenly reappeared.

I remember where and when I bought that jacket. I remember wearing it with black velvet leggings, and I remember feeling that my life would be okay when I wore that outfit. There was something about wearing the anorak, with the fur pulled up tight around my face, that made me feel safe (though sometimes the fur would get stuck in my lip gloss).

I wanted the anorak to stay, but that too was worn. The gold lining was riddled with holes. It would have to go. As in my dream, it would have to be discarded.

An entire day was absorbed in my closet cleaning ritual. In the end, I had two large trash bags full of clothing. I realized that I hadn't only faced a closet full of clothing but also all the hopes, fantasies, and accumulated emotion that had been projected onto all those purchases. Emptying that closet meant releasing those fantasies and accepting some more realistic parameters for myself. And instead of being defined by all the brands and labels that I once found myself attracted to—a definition of self through the gaze of others—I could finally be defined by my own burgeoning sense of self.

I allowed myself to cry when I finished emptying my closets, because I realized that things weren't all that bad—in fact, they were quite good. I still couldn't afford much at that moment, but I could afford a luxury that I had almost forgotten about, the luxury of my own true emotions.

So I allowed myself the luxury of tears.

Then it was time to move on.

EPILOGUE

When I started working on this book, I began to speak openly about my shopping addiction with some friends and colleagues. In doing so, I was surprised to find that almost everyone I spoke with had a story about a compulsive shopper they knew.

One friend told me about his mother who, in one of her shopping outbursts, decided to order whole roomfuls of furniture from Bloomingdale's. He retains a vivid memory of his mom standing in the driveway of their suburban home, marooned in a sea of Bloomingdale's boxes, while the delivery truck drove off into the sunset. Such outbursts, he explained, eventually ruined her credit rating.

Another story has to do with a newlywed, a trip to Saks Fifth Avenue, a personal shopper, and a credit card. Almost $50,000 worth of *ka-ching* later she left the store on a shopaholic high, only to return the next day and cancel more than half the purchases.

There was another story about a man, who couldn't keep himself from buying CDs. He had tens of thousands.

Today when I Google the words *shopping addict* or *compulsive shopper,* I am confronted with thousands of entries. The Internet is cluttered with blogs written by self-confessed shopaholics. One blogger says she is "shopping for labels, shopping for love," while another insists she's not the stereotypical "cute and stylish shopaholic" seen in movies. She is overweight, agoraphobic, and addicted to buying on eBay. Still another admits that her shopping has put enormous "stress" on her credit cards and bank account. Shopaholic blogs are filled with confessions, anguish, sadness, a touch of humor, and most often, something that sounds remarkably close to despair.

There are abundant websites offering guidance: 12-step debt management programs; "Ten Ways to Know If You Are Addicted to Credit"; and therapists, counselors, and support groups for out-of-control shoppers. There is even a shopping addiction hypnosis tape available for $19.95!

After my mother's death in 1989, when I first began to shop compulsively, none of these services existed. In fact, it would have probably been impossible for me to even put a proper name to my problem. The psychiatric term for the condition, *compulsive shopping disorder,* did not come into use until the early 1990s. Moreover, at the time, shopping was condoned as a self-congratulatory act, something to be looked on as rewarding: self-gifting, getting some retail therapy, shopping to tackle the "blues"—all became popularly used phrases. And to declare oneself a "shopaholic" elicited smiles and pats on the back, maybe even envy. This made it difficult for me to think of my shopping episodes as a problem.

Yet at some point, I knew they were.

It was not until the end of the decade that I began to see magazine articles, which addressed shopping addiction as a legitimate issue—as a compulsive disorder with potentially serious consequences, as well as both physical and psychological symptoms. Even then, the seriousness of the problem was often couched in humor.

Still, as I was completing this book, in the midst of the global financial crisis, the subjects of shopping, consumer credit, greed, and conspicuous consumption all became hot-button topics, bringing to mind the myriad images of a culture gone shopping mad. Some editorial journalists called for the American consumer to come to the rescue of the ailing economy and simply "go shopping" in order to continue to stimulate economic growth, while others were striking the death knell for the golden age of bling.

A *New York Times* article from 2008, "In Hard Times, No More Fancy Pants," suggests that showing off one's wealth has become gauche, and there is a "reconsideration of what is acceptable consumerism."

All spending habits, credit card debt, and the display of personal wealth have come into question. Frugality, a word almost unspoken in the last two decades, has suddenly reappeared. Those who are still "stealth shopping" were rumored to be brown-bagging their purchases at shops like Hermès and Louis Vuitton. The showy shop bag had lost its status.

But continuing to buy lots of stuff, even if it is disguised in a brown bag, does not reflect a true change in values. And for every report that compulsive shoppers are being reformed by the new age of austerity, there is another declaring shopping addiction is stronger than ever.

According to Karen Pine, author of *Sheconomics,* women are more inclined to spend themselves out of misery during times of crisis. Her studies reveal that some women use shopping to regulate emotions and anesthetize themselves against negative feelings.

Confusing times for a recovering shopping addict?

While I take full responsibility for my compulsive shopping habit, my poor choices, and personal debt, at times I did question how much the age in which I lived had played a role in the flourishing of my addiction. In the conclusion of her book *I Shop, Therefore I Am: Compulsive Buying and the Search for Self,* Dr. Benson poses the same question: Are consumer and culture codependent? In her essay, she queries the influence that socioeconomic and technological changes, beginning in the 1960s (the decade in which I was born), have had on shoppers. The shopping mall experience, displays of wealth on television, which made possible "a globalized desire for things," and the influence of advertising have all, writes Benson, led to an unhealthy approach to shopping and the resulting realization that "more may well be less."

My story is marked by all these changes: the advent of a mall culture, a proliferation of advertising and media influences, and a society that increasingly measured prosperity in material possessions. By the 1990s, the link between marketed goods and self-identity had become even more pronounced.

I know that fashion magazines were critical in my forming an image of myself, a female identity. My bid for perfection was based on the images of the magazine page. The magazine image was the portal to the purchase. I know that having access to easy credit aided and abetted my desire to acquire. Throughout the past three decades, credit cards became the foot soldiers of a society gone shopping mad, and I know that certain television programs exerted a pull on my psyche.

I have to admit, I was glad when the age of *Sex in the City* was over, because it sometimes felt nearly impossible to combat that illusion, even as the forces of reality were raging around me. I *was* Carrie Bradshaw! I was a freelance journalist in New York City, and I knew that on a freelance writer's salary I could not afford to have cocktails every evening and buy tons of pairs of $500 shoes. I knew that Carrie Bradshaw was a farce. Yet I bought into the illusion.

While all these outside forces exerted their pull, the key ingredients—my grief, my low self-esteem, my childish behavior toward finance—were all my own. My impulses to spend were not implanted by Saks Fifth Avenue or the editors of *Vogue*. In light of the fact that the majority of shoppers are not compulsive overspenders, do not get themselves in unmanageable debt, and do not ruin personal relationships, it may be unfair to place too much onus on society's ills.

And yet when I see fourteen-year-olds craving and coveting $1,400 handbags, or read articles that proclaim in 2010, more than half of young British women will be carrying an average credit card debt of £5,000 (about $8,000) due to out-of-control spending that comes from seeking to emulate celebrity lifestyles, I can't help but hear a warning bell. Today, compulsive shopping behavior is reported worldwide, from Italy to Australia, England to India.

Was my problem a legitimate health issue, an actual pathology, a clinical disorder? I do not have the answer for this.

As of this writing, compulsive shopping disorder remains unrecognized by the mental health profession's guidebook, the *Diagnostic and Statistical Manual of Mental Disorders,* generally called the DSM. (Currently, it is listed along with other compulsive disorders.) But this may change, since, as psychiatrists get ready to draft the next edition, due for publication in the near future, compulsive shopping disorder is being considered for inclusion.

Anticipating this, health-care professionals, academics, and researchers have been stepping up analysis and discussion as to the nature of the condition, its causes, and how widespread it may actually be.

Today, my life and my shopping habits have changed. I no longer live in the epicenter of shopping temptation, Midtown Manhattan. I moved to London, married, and then relocated to France. Not coincidentally, I ended up marrying the very man I had fallen in love with more than twenty years ago when I first came to Paris. Although geography had kept us separated at that time, we remained in contact. He is not a shopper and has never defined himself by material possessions.

Currently, we live on the west end of Paris, in a residential neighborhood. I no longer step out my front door to find a candyland of retail opportunities. This, according to the experts, is a healthy move. Creating a safe distance from triggers is half the battle.

My relationship with my family—my father and two brothers—has opened up as well. We now speak more freely about the past and even about the objects in the basement of our childhood home, a subject that now serves as a balm.

Yes, I do still shop. I still have a tendency to buy things and keep them in their bags, but I no longer hide them in the back of the closet. I hold on to them for a short while, savor their newness, and then eventually wear them. I allow myself to want something, to truly desire it, before buying it. I do not overspend nor live beyond my means.

And when I do shop, that experience is no longer marked

by peculiar physical sensations, regret, or grief. The need to fill a hole in myself—whether from a lack in earliest childhood, my mother's death, or poor self-esteem—is no longer there.

I have tried in the pages of this book to highlight some of the real perils of overspending, of trying to appear to be well-off when I was not, of ignoring my financial health in the process, and of harming relationships. However, more important, I have tried to highlight the dangers of living in a manner that negated my essence. In denying my emotional needs, I was almost literally disappearing. And when I asked myself the question—*How can a woman with a closet so full feel so utterly empty inside?*—it wasn't without genuine sadness and confusion. Truthfully, there was a time when I did not know how to begin to answer that question.

While I know my story is not the most dramatic, nor my perils as daunting or dangerous as some others I have since heard about, I also know that my experiences strike this familiar shopping addict chord: trying to replace a lack of internal substance with external artifice.

Today, for me, shopping is no longer about filling an internal void. And that has made all the difference.

ACKNOWLEDGMENTS

Thank you to my agent, and friend, John Ware, for your patience, encouragement, and humor.

Thank you to my fabulous editor, Judy Clain, for your enthusiasm from the start and your insightful observations and suggestions.

Thank you to the entire Little, Brown team: Michael, Nathan, Elizabeth, Amanda T., Amanda B., Tracy, Peggy, and everyone else. Thank you for your professionalism and kindness.

Thank you to Dr. April Benson for sharing your expertise and interest in my story.

Thank you to all my girlfriends, with special thanks to Kim, Meg, Christa, Haysun, and Alicia for your wisdom and advice.

Thank you to my family: Dad, August, and Frank. Thank you for being the home to which I can always return.

Thank you, most of all, to Tim, my husband, *l'homme de ma vie*. Thank you for your unwavering love. Thank you for your warm meals to nourish me and your strong arms to protect me, and for providing an endless supply of perfect *bon mots* whenever I found myself at a loss for words.

NOTES

Two: Oniomania and Me

The letter from Jacqueline Kennedy appears in *The Eloquent Jacqueline Kennedy Onassis: A Portrait in Her Own Words* by Bill Adler.

Adler, Bill. *The Eloquent Jacqueline Kennedy Onassis.* New York: HarperCollins, 2004.

"Buying is much more American than thinking and I'm as American as they come" is the opening sentence of Warhol's essay "Underwear Power," which appears in a collection of Warhol's musings on everything from food, sex, and fame to art and, of course, shopping. The essay recalls a Saturday morning shopping trip to Macy's to purchase underwear. As Warhol arrives at Macy's, he describes the people pouring into the department store as all having buying "in their blood and minds and eyes."

Warhol, Andy. *The Philosophy of Andy Warhol (From A to B and Back Again).* New York: Harcourt Brace Jovanovich, 1975.

My original copy of *Cheap Chic* still sits on my bookshelf. To leaf through its pages is to see how much the language of style has changed in the past thirty-five years. Hardly a brand name or designer label is mentioned in its pages. The book originally sold for $5.95. Today, copies are selling for up to several hundred dollars on auction sites such as eBay.

Milinaire, Caterine, and Carol Troy. *Cheap Chic: Hundreds of Money Saving Hints to Create Your Own Great Look.* New York: Crown, 1975.

Joyce Carol Oates's story "Shopping" is included in the book *Heat and Other Stories.*

Oates, Joyce Carol. *Heat and Other Stories.* New York: Plume, 1992.

Three: Charged Up

In *The Overspent American: Why We Want What We Don't Need,* Juliet Schor highlights many of the social factors that are believed to contribute to compulsive spending. Among them are increased job pressures that result in compensatory purchasing, the ubiquity of shopping opportunities, measuring oneself against affluent groups, and the desire to maintain an image of success.

Schor, Juliet. *The Overspent American: Why We Want What We Don't Need.* New York: HarperPerennial, 1999.

Five: Material World

Schor, Juliet. "The New Politics of Consumption." *The Boston Review* 34, nos. 3–4 (1999): 4–9. Among the many salient points made in this essay is Schor's admonition that "somebody needs to be for quality of life, not just quantity of stuff."

Six: Fashions of the Times

Ellis, Bret Easton. *Glamorama.* New York: Knopf, 1998.
McInerney, Jay. *Model Behavior.* New York: Knopf, 1998.

Both of these novels were published when the cult of celebrity, status, getting and spending, and luxury-label fever reached their peak.

Seven: The Price of Everything, the Value of Nothing

Benson, April Lane. *I Shop, Therefore I Am: Compulsive Buying and the Search for Self.* Plymouth, UK: Jason Aronson, 2000.

At the time of its publication in July, 2000, this was the only book of its kind: a comprehensive study of compulsive buying that addressed both the root causes and treatment options for what was often referred to as the "smiled upon" addiction.

Dr. Black's research is included in his detailed report "A Review of Compulsive Buying Disorder," a succinct profile of the compulsive shopping personality.

Black, Donald W. "A Review of Compulsive Buying Disorder," *World Psychiatry* 6, no. 1 (2007): 14–18.

Being and Nothingness: An Essay on Phenomenological Ontology by Jean-Paul Sartre, originally published in French in 1943, is considered his most significant philosophical work. In addition to this book, I have been influenced by Jean Baudrillard's writings about objects and their meaning in *The System of Objects*, originally published in French in 1968.

Sartre, Jean-Paul. *L'Être et le néant: Essai d'ontologie phénoménologique.* Paris: Librairie Gallimard, 1943.

Baudrillard, Jean. *Le Système des objects.* Paris: Editions Gallimard, 1968.

Ten: Better to Shop Than Pray

In the past few years, myriad articles on the burgeoning fields of neuroeconomics and neuromarketing have appeared. Among those I read during the course of writing this book were "Inside the Shopping Brain" by Sharon Begley and "This Is Your Brain on Shopping" by Nikhil Swaminathan.

Begley, Sharon. "Inside the Shopping Brain." *Newsweek* (December 15, 2008).

Swaminathan, Nikhil. "This Is Your Brain on Shopping." *Scientific American* (January 5, 2007).

Twelve: Loss and Lost

Craik, Jennifer. *The Face of Fashion: Cultural Studies in Fashion.* New York: Routledge, 1994.

Craik's book offers an in-depth analysis of the way identity is projected through clothing and the role that the fashion industry and fashion images play in that process.

Bordo, Susan. *Twilight Zones: The Hidden Life of Cultural Images from Plato to O.J.* Berkeley: University of California Press, 1997.

In this text, Bordo presents an analysis of the cultural influence of images.

Fourteen: After the Fall

In *Why We Shop: Emotional Rewards and Retail Strategies,* Jim Pooler highlights the emotional and psychological motivations of the modern shopper.

Pooler, Jim. *Why We Shop: Emotional Rewards and Retail Strategies.* Westport: Praeger Publishers, 2003.

In *The Soul of the New Consumer* by David Lewis and Darren Bridger, the authors examine modern consumers' quest for authenticity both in themselves and in the purchases they make.

Lewis, David, and Darren Bridger. *The Soul of the New Consumer.* London: Nicholas Brealey Publishing, 2001.

Epilogue

In *Sheconomics* by Karen Pine and Simonne Gnessen, the authors explore women's emotional relationships with money and propose seven laws of "sheconomics" to help them take control of their financial futures.

Pine, Karen, and Simonne Gnessen. *Sheconomics.* London: Headline, 2009.

ABOUT THE AUTHOR

After spending her formative years reading fashion magazines voraciously, Avis Cardella found her calling writing about photography, fashion, and culture. She has written for British *Vogue,* *American Photo,* and *Surface,* among other publications. She lives in Paris with her husband.